REAL

WORKING
DRAWINGS

DIY HOUSE PLANS
USING *FREE* SOFTWARE

MONOLITHIC DOME EDITION
...APPLICABLE TO ANY HOUSE STYLE

FROM 3D MODEL TO THE FINAL SET
OF DRAWINGS AND BEYOND...
EVERYTHING YOU NEED TO KNOW

by Robert Bissett

Meadow Creek Editions

Dedication

To those who have miraculously survived natural disasters
without benefit of properly designed and built structures.
To those who tragically lost loved ones and possessions
when it could have been prevented.
To those who played the odds in a wood frame building and lost.
To those who believed government, building codes, insurance
companies, mortgage lenders or builders would protect them.
To those who say 'never again' and are looking for a better way.

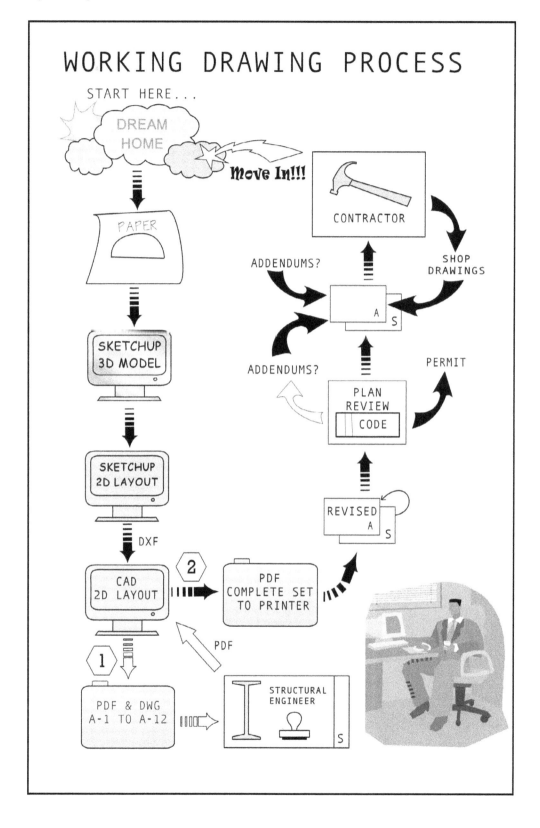

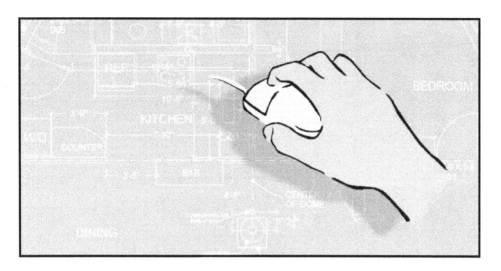

TABLE of CONTENTS

A recent proposal for a hotel done in SketchUp.

FOREWORD

Robert Bissett is a very special individual, whose knowledge and expertise include both art and architecture. For the past eight years, it has been my privilege to work with him on projects involving Monolithic Domes, non-traditional, ultra-green, disaster-resistant structures first introduced thirty-five years ago. Since then, hundreds of privately and publicly owned Monolithic Domes have been built and are in use worldwide.

In 2004, Robert received the 2004 Projects of Distinction Merit Award for the design of Paul and Barbara Stitt's Monolithic Dome home in Manitowoc, Wisconsin. Robert visited the site and began the design in December of 1998. He delivered the final drawings in July 2001. This luxurious dome-home, overlooking Lake Michigan, has a diameter of 55 feet and three spacious, beautifully finished levels.

Robert also collaborated on the design of Dome of a Home in Pensacola Beach, Florida. This 3,400-square-foot Monolithic Dome made national headlines when it emerged virtually unscathed from a direct hit by Hurricane Ivan, and later, just as successfully survived Hurricane Dennis.

Robert's book Real Working Drawings is a tool people can use to help them draw their own dome plans. In it, Robert shares his knowledge of how to use the programs and draw blueprints without spending a fortune. The book includes all the tricks of the trade.

Robert Bissett is a man ahead of his time, who is trying to help the rest of the world catch up. I thank him for allowing me to write this Foreword.

David B. South,
President, Monolithic Dome Institute

INTRODUCTION

What's Covered

You have spent months going over the plan for your new Monolithic dome. You know the spaces your dream house will have and just how it should be laid out. You have gone as far as you can with pencil and paper. Rather than turn all your sketches and notes over to a professional you would prefer to do the working drawings yourself. By doing it yourself you can continue to refine your design, you can consult with the contractors who will be doing the actual work benefiting from their good ideas and experience and saving money. If you have the interest, some computer skills and are willing to spend the time, this book can be your guide to a rewarding experience and a very useable and professional looking set of working drawings, all with software available free on the internet. You will find the actual files depicted in this book on my website for downloading and further study. They will give you a huge head start on your own project. Only one line weight will be used.

Any design process has to accommodate mistakes, changes, better ideas and new information. I have treated this just like a real project for a real client. I've left some of the false starts in for you to see rather than make it look like a completely smooth road from beginning to end.

What's not Covered

This book will not teach you how to use a computer. Nor will it teach you how to use any software or how to navigate the internet. Neither is this book about how to design a practical, pleasant and livable dome home, nor how to push the limits of dome design. This book does not deal with green design, or alternate energy, or storm surge design for coastal areas. Nor do I come close to revealing all the amazing things that can be done with SketchUp or Monolithic Domes. Nor do I employ LayOut, the companion program to SketchUp.

The Computer.

My introduction to computers occurred in the early sixties when I was a cadet at the USAF Academy. I sat at a terminal and produced a stack of punch cards. When I was certain they were perfect, they never were, I handed them to a technician through a window. In a day or so the printout would be ready. I usually had many errors to track down and fix. We were never allowed into the climate controlled room that housed the huge computer itself. It was the very latest thing. No one had even imagined a home computer. Now, nearly fifty years later, we have amazingly powerful machines you can carry under your arm. Combined with the internet they have replaced the typewriter, the printing press, the darkroom, the Post Office, the library and much more. Likely your present computer, if it is fairly new, can handle the software recommended here. Verify system requirements to be sure.

The Software.

Using computers for design often requires two or more programs and a way to transfer files between them. House design is no different. To pick up where SketchUp leaves off you will need several free programs. After trying many CAD programs, I recommend DraftSight offered by Dassaults Systemes. In addition you will want a photo editing program like the free Gimp to enhance 3D views. A second free CAD program, DoubleCAD XT, will be required to produce successfully a set of pdf sheets. The free version of Wintopo for making vector drawings from jpgs will be useful as will several plugins available for SketchUp. Plus the word processing program called Abiword can be had at no cost online. Links to all these programs can be found on my website. If you have TurboCAD, Paint Shop, Word or other commercial software, all the better. Only the PC with MS Windows operating system is covered here, but Sketchup is available in a Mac version and the process is very similar.

I looked far and wide trying to find a better deal than SketchUp for modeling. Bonzai3D is as good but has no drafting capabilities and is expensive. I recommend the SketchUp free version. It is the most intuitive 3D modeling program available. The paid Pro version costing around five hundred dollars comes with a separate program called LayOut for layout and drafting. LayOut has gotten better but still has a ways to go. LayOut can not import common vector file formats and has a number of other shortcomings. I have the pro version. You can spend the big bucks on the Pro version and probably do a fair job on working drawings. But there is no need. You can use the free version plus the tips and tricks you will find in this book.

Step 1: The Model

You will first make a SketchUp 3D model. Building the dome digitally for practice before the real, and expensive, construction phase is well worth doing. Working with full sized 1:1 objects you will discover problems and solve them. It is easy to change a computer model; much harder to change concrete and steel. Later, if you need to add a detail it is easy to extract the basic lines and export them to your CAD program for drafting, dimensions and text. You can quickly determine if the new location for the ceiling fan over the stairs, for example, provides enough head room.

SketchUp is intended to be a tool for quick modeling of concepts in 3D. It can also be used to make accurate models and drawings very much like a CAD program. It can not make true circles, arcs or curves. Instead it makes all curves from a number of straight segments. SketchUp has a text tool which makes words from line segments which can not be edited as text in SketchUp or when exported to a CAD program. The Label Tool makes editable text, but it doesn't export at all.

The best way to save time and effort is to make the model precise at each step. It only takes a little extra care to do it right.

Step 2: The Visualization

A major benefit of a 3D model is the opportunity to see what your house will look like from every angle both inside and out before it is built. In this book the focus is working drawings. On a short detour you will learn how to create an exterior and an interior rendering. Starting with a SketchUp image you will use a photo editing program to bring it to life.

Not everything SketchUp does can be covered here. You can try variations in shape and size. Investigate a range of materials, colors and furniture. Design your own furniture. Design your kitchen and bath. You can model your actual building site and preview your landscaping. Do solar studies. See how it all will look from the street. Model your neighborhood. Get the feel of that great room. Do a fly by or a walk through. You can do photo realistic renderings with the help of yet another free program.

Step 3: The Airform

Be sure your airform can be inflated as you expect. Check with Monolithic, Inc. in Italy, Texas prior to beginning the model just to be sure. Send them your initial dome section and proposed openings. When ordering the airform send the opening/dome section drawing sheet to Monolithic.

Step 4: Plan Review

Working drawings are not created in a vacuum. Many factors must be considered. Some are financial: how much do you want to spend and can you get financing. Some are legal: Building codes, zoning, covenants. The structural engineer has a major role. You will almost certainly need a building permit. Early on you will want to get a copy of the local permit package with it's checklist of items required in your drawings.

Step 5: Sheets, Title Blocks & Borders

We'll do a mockup of all the sheets in SketchUp beginning with the sheet size, half inch border and title block.

Step 6: 3D to 2D

With the help of a few free plugins and a free raster to vector converter, you will be able to extract from the model all the necessary vector drawings or jpg images.

Step 7: The Preliminary Layout

Do as much of the layout as you can in SketchUp. Create a mock up of the final set of working drawings that will show with space holders what is needed and which sheet it will go on. This will include space for word processing documents, jpgs, drawings, details and text.

Step 8: The Finished Layout

When you have taken it as far as possible in SketchUp you will export your preliminary sheet layouts in a standard CAD format called .dxf, Drawing Exchange Format. That file will then be opened in a DraftSight to add drafting, text, dimensions and fills. You will also add the images created in SketchUp using the referencing feature of the CAD program. Referencing will also be used to add the word processing documents.

Step 9: Structural Engineering

Once completely assembled and finalized save each sheet as a vector .pdf. This must be done in a round about manner. Open the DraftSight dwg in DoubleCAD XT, print each sheet as a pdf. Now it's time to send the set of pdfs and the native DraftSight .dwg file to the structural engineer. The engineer will produce his own set of sheets showing how the dome must be constructed. He will also deal with the ringbeam, other footings, columns, floor joists and so on. He will use your CAD file as the basis for his drawings.

Step 10: The Complete Set

Once you have studied the pdf structural sheets update your drawings to conform to the engineer's if necessary. Convert your final corrected sheets to pdf. Send your sheets along with the engineer's to your local printer by email. Deliver a printed set to the plan reviewer. If any changes or additions are required they can probably be handled with just an addendum.

Step 11: Addendums

If changes, additions, corrections or clarifications to the drawings are needed you may issue addendums to the plan holders which become a part of the contract documents. Words alone may be enough or a drawing may also be required.

Step 12: Shop Drawings

In several places on the working drawings shop drawings will be called for. This gives the dome constructor and contractor the opportunity to employ the newest and best materials and methods, or those most familiar. It could be that the contractor submits a hand drawn sketch of his idea. To save time and money and to avoid any confusion you may want to draft up his drawing to scale yourself for his signature.

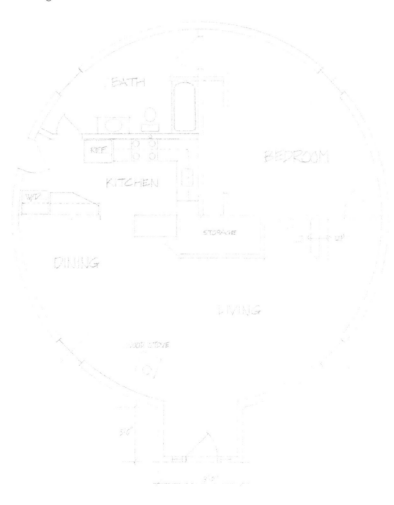

Original pencil on paper floor plan sketch

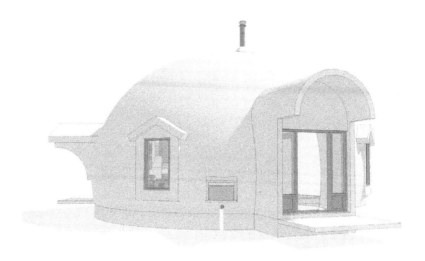

Completed SketchUp model.

Step 1: The Model

The easiest and least expensive way to make a set of working drawings is by doing as much as possible in the amazing, free Google SketchUp program. It's not the only way. You could draw them by hand with pencil and paper. You could also use a CAD program, either 2D or 3D.

You could use the 3D architecture specific program I have used for many domes called ArchiCAD. A pleasure to use for layout and drafting it is no match for SketchUp for modeling. Far from free, it costs around four thousand dollars.

Configure Sketchup.

Select the Engineering Style, Parallel projection, Hidden Line or Shaded, Profile Edges optional and Shadows off, axis on. Palettes – most of them with the heading visible ready to be dropped down and most of the tools visible.

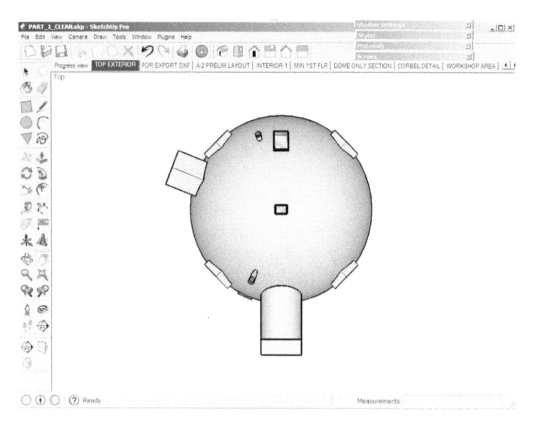

Install these plugins: Import DXF, Export to Dxf or Stl, Flatten to Plane. Links to these can be found in Resources at the end of the book.

1. The Shells

The heart of any dome home is the dome. Start by constructing the dome with two shells, an inner and an outer. You could make the dome all at once, but you will later need the shells to be separate groups on separate layers. Let's assume you have in mind a weekend retreat thirty-six feet in diameter with a second floor loft covering half the first floor.

First draw a section of the dome. Draw a circle with seventy-two segments and a diameter of thirty-six feet. Add a vertical dimension with the Dimension tool from the center of the circle to the highest point. It should read 18'.

The plan is for an oblate spheroid, but how flat should it be? The ratio of semi-major axis to semi-minor axis, or ellipticity, is moderate at 1.35 and highly elliptical at 1.45. For this dome moderate would be 13'-4" and we would not normally go lower than this. The plan is to raise the equator of the dome 3'-6" so that all the floor space is useable. That gives us an overall height of 16'-10". That sounds too low for two stories. A four inch slab will reduce it further. Our best guess at this point is 19' overall height for the dome. Less 3'-6" leaves 15'-6" from the equator or beltline, an ellipticity of 18'/15.6' = 1.16, well within limits.

An accurate ellipse. Add a dimension from the center to the top of the circle. Select the face of the circle and using the Scale tool, scale vertically as close as possible to 15'-6" and click. You won't hit it exactly. The closest I could get was 15'-5 3/4" at .86 or 86 percent. Close in on the exact value by entering numbers in the Measurement Toolbar until you find the percentage that produces 15'-6". I found that .8610 works after a couple tries. But, these further attempts also gave 15'-6": .8611 and .8612; .8613 and .8609 did not work. Go with the middle value of .8611.

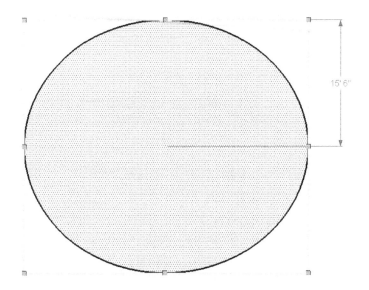

Draw a short horizontal line from the center of the ellipse. Draw a vertical line 3'-6" down from that line. Below the ellipse draw a line a little wider than the ellipse. Drag that line straight up to make the bottom of the shell. Almost any other way of making this bottom line will cause trouble. It is important that when you select the arc for the shell that the entire arc is selected all at once. If you find you must make two or more selections to get the entire arc, undo and try again. The multiple selections will be a problem when it's time to revolve the 3D shell. I think this way is fool proof.

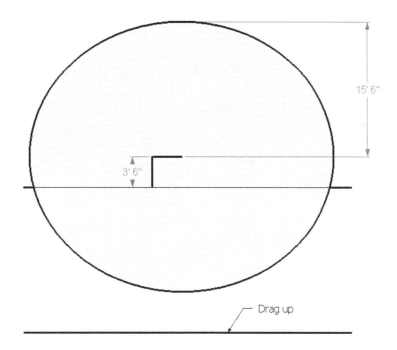

Drag/Copy the full arc to use for our dome section drawing. Draw a vertical line from the center to the top of the ellipse. Select the left hand half of the curve and Drag/Copy it over to the left. This curve will be used to make the outer 3D shell. Drag it to a safe place where you can find it.

You want the dome wall to be 7" thick at the bottom tapering to 6" thick at the top. Subtracting 3" for the foam insulation leaves 4" of concrete at the bottom and 3" at the top. That is our best guess for what the engineer will require. If your dome is a different size, ask your engineer what wall thickness to use for design purposes. Repeat the above steps to make an ellipse for the inner shell that is 34'-10" wide and 15'-0" high. Drag/Copy the two arcs as before. Also Drag/Copy the bottom line of each shell. These are small than the equator diameters and will be used later to make the circles needed to revolve the 3D shells.

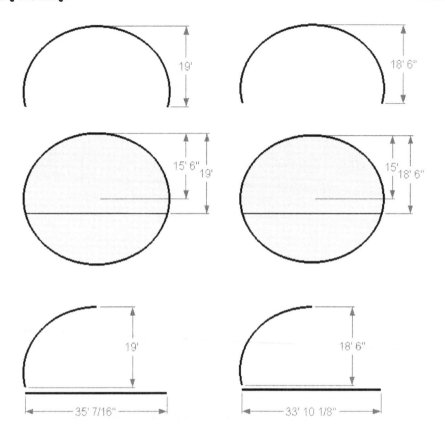

Combine the two full arcs to make a section through the middle of the dome. Be sure they are positioned accurately by the use of center points.

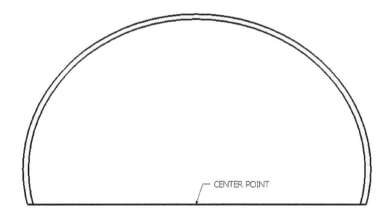

CENTER POINT

Now make a line at the 8' level for the top of the first floor wall, a line 10" above that for the second floor level. Add a line six feet above that to check head room and useable floor space. Notice that placing the equator at 3'-6" makes the entire first floor useable up to seven feet for kitchen cabinets and furniture. Group and save this. It will be useful later.

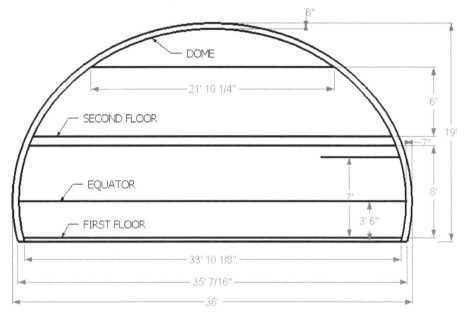

Time to make the 3D shells. Add two lines to the shell arcs to form two faces. Make a circle with 48 segments for both base diameters. You will later use 48 segment circles to make the floor slab and the foundation ringbeam. Align the bottoms of the two arcs and the middles of the two circles.

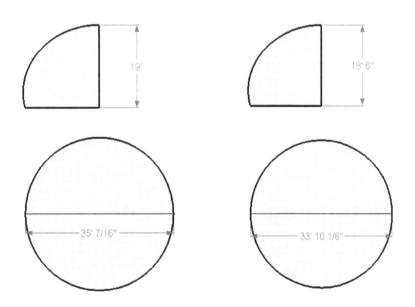

Rotate both arc faces ninety degrees up and center them on their respective circles. If you lined them up first you can rotate and center both at the same time. Delete the face of the circle and add a two foot vertical handle to the top of each arc. Rotate the view so you can see the bottom of the arc. Use the Follow me tool on the outer arc face. It will follow the circle and revolve a dome shell. Repeat all these steps for the inner shell.

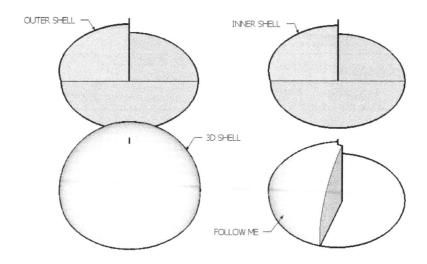

Select the bottom circular face under both 3D shells formed along with the shells. Drag/Copy them. These will be used to make the ringbeam and floor slab. Delete the bottom face of the outer 3D shell and select the shell and the handle on top. Create a component and call it Shell Outer. Create a Layer and call it Shell Outer. Place the shell on this new layer. Repeat for the inner 3D shell. Make a set of center lines along the three major directions. Group them and call it Center Lines. Make a new layer called Center Lines and place the group on that layer. This will aid in keeping things straight and properly aligned throughout the project.

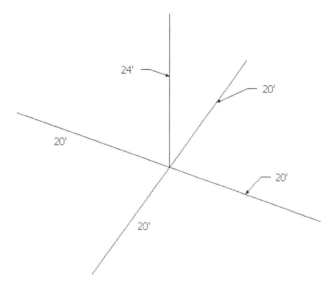

Using the handles position both shells centered on the vertical line with the bottoms on the horizontal lines. Congratulations! You have completed the dome. Make sure you have everything the right size and in the exact location before proceeding.

2. Ringbeam & Floor Slab

Ringbeam. The dome's foundation is called the ringbeam. The structural engineer will size the dome shell, the ringbeam and other structural parts, but you will take an educated guess. Let's make the ringbeam 18" x 18". On the larger circle from the bottom of the outer 3D shell we just made, create an offset of 18". Add a rectangle for the entry 8' x 5' with an 18" offset. Remove the extra lines and Push/Pull the face down 18". Make a two foot handle in the middle in the down direction. Make a group called Ringbeam from the ringbeam and handle. Make a layer of the same name for that group. Move the Ringbeam into place under the dome.

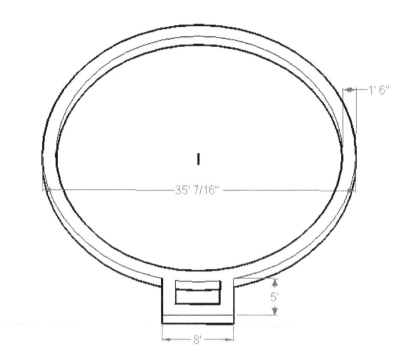

Floor Slab. To the bottom circle from the inner shell add a rectangle 7' x 5' for the entry. Remove extra lines. Push/Pull upward 4". Add a downward handle in the middle. Make a group called Floor Slab. Make a layer of the same name for that group. Move the slab into position on top of the ringbeam.

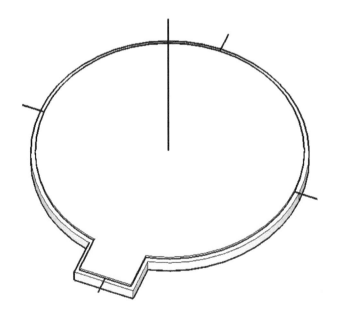

How is yours looking? When you have the model accurate and perfectly located go on to the next section and give yourself a pat on the back.

3. Walls

The original idea was to have a wall dividing the dome exactly in half with another wall ninety degrees to that between the bedroom and bath/kitchen. It looks ok in the pencil drawing, so that is where we will start. Walls will be 8' high and built with 3 ½" steel studs and ½" sheetrock on both sides for a total of 4 ½". The plumbing wall will be built with 5 ½" studs for a total of 6 ½". Following the pencil drawing, construct these walls.

Draw a horizontal line in the middle of the floor slab. Drag the line up 2 ¼". Drag/Copy that line down 4 ½". Ninety degrees to that and in the middle make two more lines 4 ½" apart. Add Construction Lines for the closet and plumbing wall between the Bath and Kitchen.

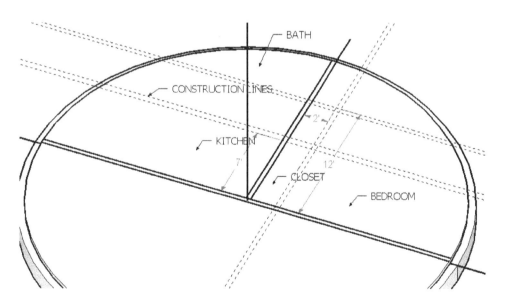

A good start, however, I wonder if there is room in the Bath for a five foot tub, a 4 ½" wall and a 3'-0" door. And will that door fully open without hitting the dome wall? Let's investigate before going further.

Make a new layer called Plumbing. Build a minimal tub 5'-0"L x 32"W x 16"H. Group and label it Tub and place it on the new layer. Make a new layer called

Doors. Build a 3'-0"x 6'-8" door panel with a two inch frame. Group the panel and frame and call it 3-0x6-8, placing it on the new layer.

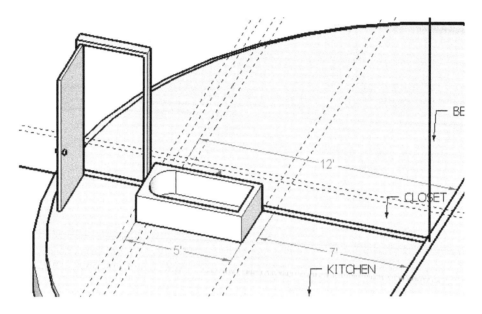

It should be able to open a full 90 degrees. You can check by making the Inner Shell layer visible and using a vertical Section Plane.

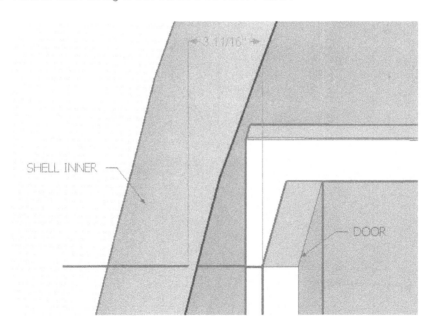

By drawing a line from the corner of the door through the shell and applying a dimension you see it has over three inches of clearance when open 90 degrees. That should be enough. Put in the rest of the lines for the walls. Add end caps to each wall and remove extra lines. There should now be a face filling all the walls. Push/Pull that face 8' up.

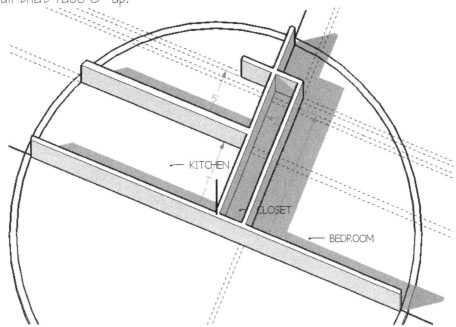

Group these walls and call it Walls 1st Floor. Make a layer of the same name for that group. A plugin is available that adds a wall tool to the program. I'm not sure it's worth the effort, especially on a small project. Two things need attention. Extend the walls horizontally beyond the equator prior to trimming them with the Inner Shell. And the plumbing wall needs to meet the dome a 90 degree angle.

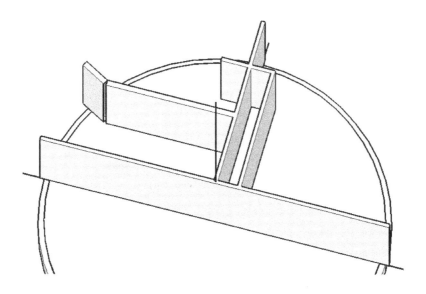

Don't fill in the bent part of the plumbing wall until you find out if the door in that wall will fit. Make the Inner Shell visible. Edit the wall group. Select all the walls. Right click on the selection, Intersect Faces > With Model. Delete the trimmed parts.

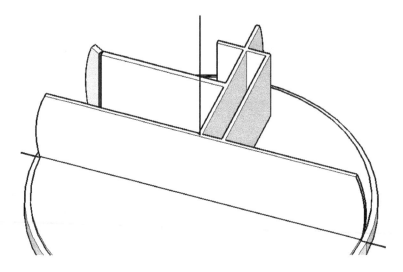

Make visible the Door layer and edit the wall group. Make an outline around the three sides of the Bath door frame. For this door you only had to draw two lines because the corner with the closet provides the third line. Push/Pull the resulting face 4 ½" to the back side of the wall. An opening appears in the wall. The door can be visible during this procedure.

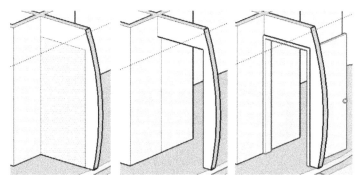

Repeat these steps for the 3-0 Bedroom door and the 2-6 Bathroom door from the Laundry. You also need a 7'-10" opening between the Kitchen and the Dining area starting 2'-1" from the Kitchen wall. An exposed beam will be added later in that opening to hold up floor joists. Add an 8'w x 7'h opening in the Bedroom closet wall for a door.

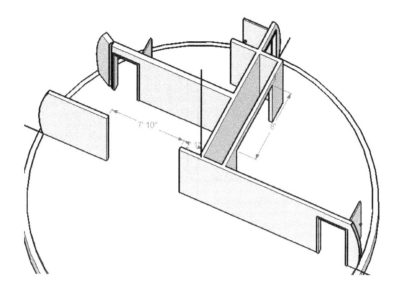

4. Second Floor

The second floor will include floor joist, rim joist, plywood subfloor, dome corbel, and beam. Make a profile for an engineered wood joist. How do you know what size joist to plan on? Measure from the inner face of the center wall stud to the inner shell. It measures 16'-3 ½" less 6" for the corbel leaves a 15'-9" span. Refer to the Residential Floor Plan Tables you will find on page four of the Western Specifier Guide, Boise Cascade website, bc.com. The BCI 5000 1.7, 9.5" H will span 17' and give us almost Three Star performance.

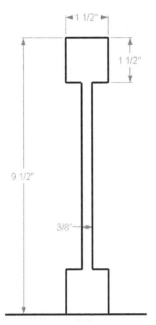

Push/Pull the face to a length of 20'. Place the joist on a new layer called Floor Joists. Position the joist on top of the first floor wall at the center of the dome. Drag/Copy the joist 16" on center covering the entire floor. Group all the joists together on the Floor Joists layer. With inner shell visible trim the joists and delete excess portions.

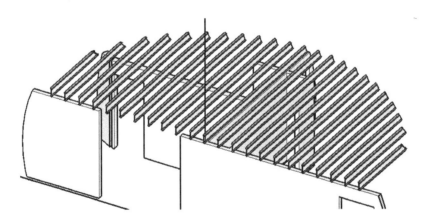

Now, make a wood beam 3 ½" x 11 ¼" for the unsupported joists. Call the group Beam Kitchen and place it on the Beam layer. Make a ¾" deck for the second floor. Make a group of this called Floor 2nd Plywd on a new layer of the same name.

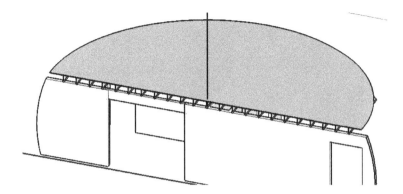

The corbel will be part of the dome in real life, but we will make it separate.
Return to the 2d dome section you drew in Step 1. Make an outline for the
corbel.

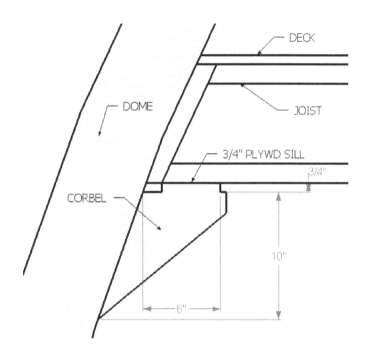

Drag/Copy the corbel and create a group called corbel, placing it on a layer called
Corbel. Make a new horizontal face with the Rectangle tool, 40' x 40'. Group and
center the square on the dome and position it at the bottom tip of the corbel
profile.

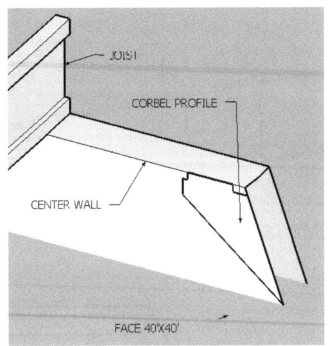

When you trimmed the walls with the inner shell the top face of the walls took on the shape of the shell which has 48 segments, and is not a smooth curve. Find where the segments of the inner shell meet at the center line of the dome.

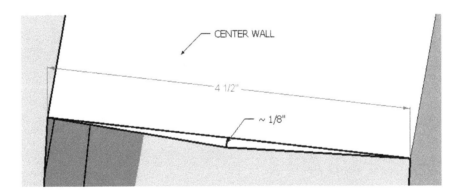

Drag/Copy the ~1/8" line to the 40'x40' face.

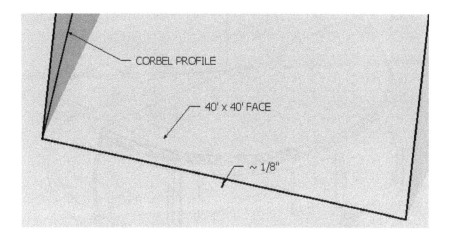

Drag/Copy the short line to the other end of the wall and to the end of the center wall ninety degrees to this wall, between the Bedroom and Bath. Now you can use the Arc tool to place a half circle with 24 segments on the 40' x 40' face. Delete all the extra lines. Turn off the first floor wall and double click to Edit the corbel profile. Use the Follow Me tool to create the 3D corbel.

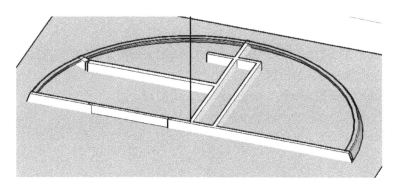

Now delete the 40' x 40' face. Both floors are done! Celebrate with your favorite beverage.

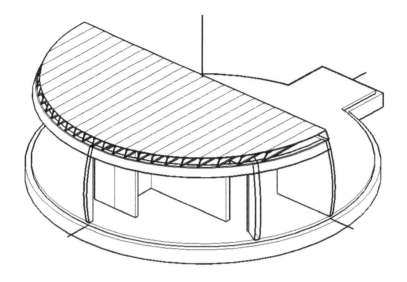

5. Stairs

Stair making plugins can be found on the internet as well as models, but let's make our own. The floor to floor distance is 8'-10 ¼". Start by drawing that line on the horizontal plane. Make a 3' x ¾" rectangle at the top for the landing. Drop down 7" and make an 11" x 1 ½" rectangle for a tread. Push/Pull both rectangles 3'. Group the landing and make a component of the tread.

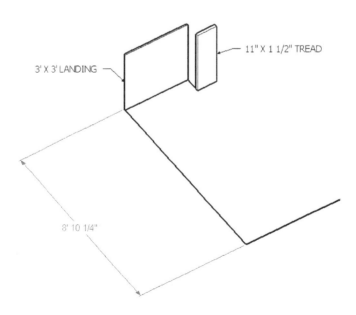

3' X 3' LANDING

11" X 1 1/2" TREAD

8' 10 1/4"

Drag the tread to the left 1" for nosing and tread of 10". Drag/Copy the tread by clicking first on the top corner of the landing and then the top corner of the tread so that the new tread is in the correct position. Type in X13 to automatically create all the treads. You want the risers to have the same height. The lowest riser is 8 ¼".

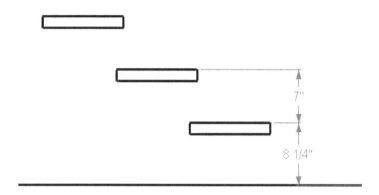

We must make an adjustment. Leaving these two riser dimensions in place, select all the treads. Activate the Scale tool. Click on the bottom center handle and pull downward till the Measurement Bar reads 1.01. Enter values until the 7" dimension and the 8 ¼" read the same. At 1.013 both read 7 1/16". The top riser is still 7" and that is acceptable.

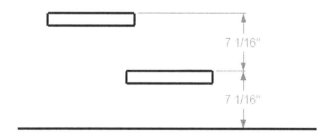

On to the stringers. You can use a grouped face on the end of the treads or a Workplane as I have here.

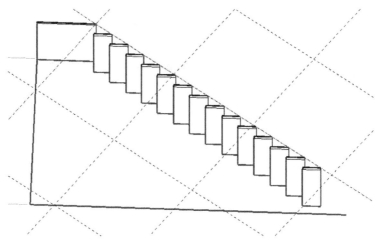

Make a stringer to support the treads and make a group. This one is 3 ½" x 14". At the landing it will be trimmed two inches to be even with the top of the deck.

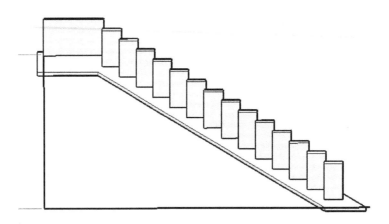

Now Drag/Copy the stringer to the other side, group the stairs placing them on a new layer called Stairs, rotate upright and move into position. Notice two beams have been added to support the stairs.

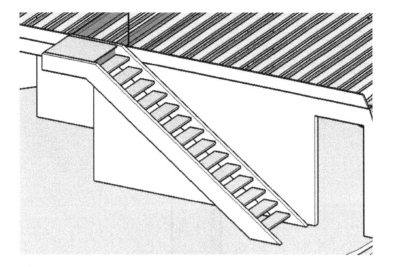

Make uprights for the handrail: Uprights for the landing are similar with a height of 34".

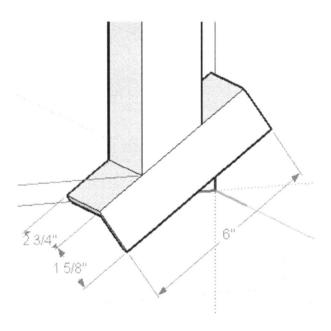

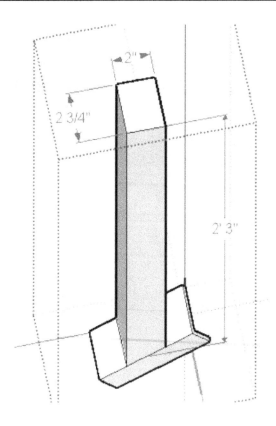

Carefully position these along the outer stringer. Use the Follow Me tool to make the handrail following a line along the tops of the uprights and ending in a half circle.

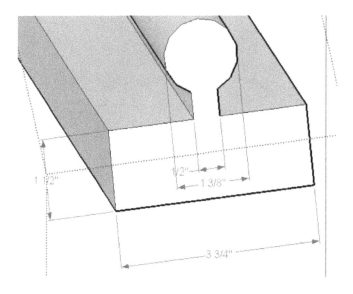

The space above and below the glass is 4". A beautiful custom design in aluminum with wood treads.

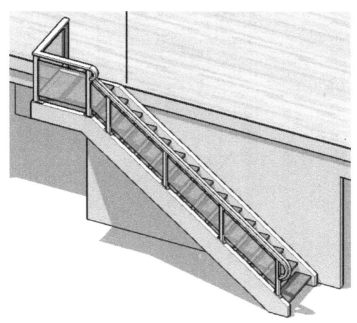

The completed stair with glass panels in place.

6. Side Door

The dome will have two doors, the main entrance and a side door off the kitchen. Starting with the side door, position a copy of the 3-0x6-8 door with frame. Make Unique the copy and add a window.

You will make an opening in the dome for this door. Make a box on the door frame the same size as the outside of the frame. Make a group called Cutter Door Side on a new layer called Dome Cutters.

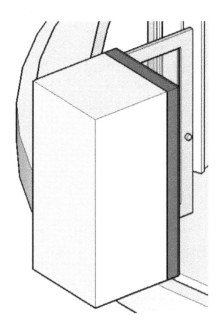

Move this cutter toward the center of dome so that it protrudes inside and outside of both dome shells and is still aligned with the door frame perfectly. Use mid-points of the upper edges.

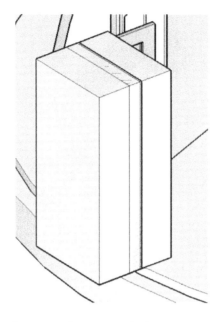

Turn off all but the Dome Cutters layer and the outer shell. Edit the shell triple clicking to select all faces and lines. Intersect Faces > With Model. Turn off the Cutters layer and delete the door shape from the shell. Leave edit mode and turn on the door layer.

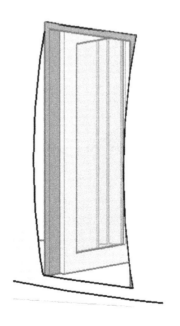

You will need to close that gap. Now cut an opening in the inner shell using the same method. You see another gap at the top of the door frame.

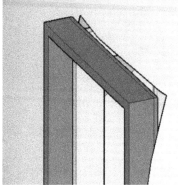

Make another box like the door cutter. Group it and place on the Shell Inner layer. Turn on only the two shells. Move the new box so that it extends on both sides of the shells. Edit the box, triple clicking to select all. Then Intersect Faces > With Model. Turn off the shells.

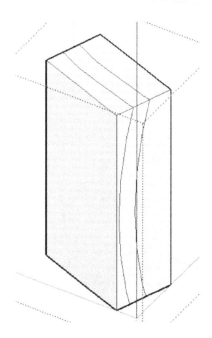

Remove the unwanted parts and the gaps are closed. Build a covered landing for the side door similar to the one below. Trim the roof and its beams with the outer shell. Later I decide to replace the posts and beams with braces.

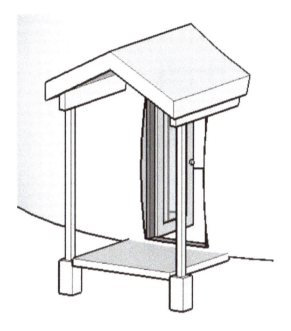

7. Main Entry

In the Top View make the shape below. Drag/Copy and using the Offset tool add the other lines. Note the bottom line has been moved down 2" to leave 4" for the floor slab. The first shape will become the cutter, the second the entry. Group each one after deleting any dimensions and place the first on the Dome Cutters layer and the second on a new layer called Entry.

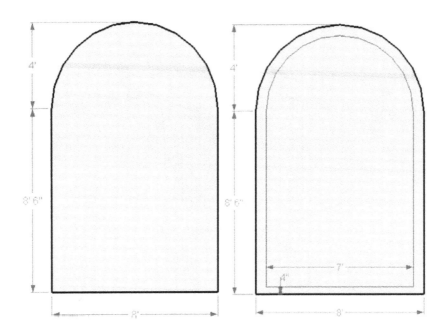

Push/Pull the walls into existence 9'. Then do the overhang another 3'. Move the front back 4" and Drag/Copy a second face 6" behind that. Make a 3'-6" x 7'-0" door with glass and sidelights. The total width of the door unit is 7' by 7'-2" high.

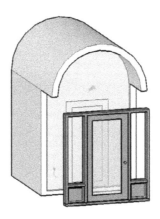

Make an opening for the door unit and move it into place. All this should be on the Entry layer with appropriately named groups. Move the entry assembly into place on the ringbeam.

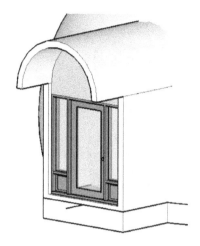

Next you will cut the opening for the entry. It will be more complicated than the side door. You'll need two cutters this time, one for the inner shell and one for the outer shell, plus the entry itself needs to be trimmed. Follow these steps remove trimmings as you go:

1.   Turn off everything but the entry and inner shell layers. Trim the entry with the inner shell.

2.   Now trim the inner shell with a cutter the same size as the interior of the entry. Extend the bottom of that cutter to the bottom of the shell.

3.   Trim the outer shell with the entry.

4.   Edit the entry manually trimming about 3" off the outside wall and curved top so that an unwanted line will not show from the inside. Use the Offset tool for the sides. For the curved top use the arc tool. First click on the top of the trimmed wall on one side, then on the other side, then the top of the curved part as shown below. Add a horizontal line at the bottom of the arc to make a face appear. Scale the face so it will overlap the curved roof. Turn off the dome shells. Rotate if necessary to trim only 2" or 3". Trim the top curved surface of the roof and remove the edge. Delete the arc face. That's it!

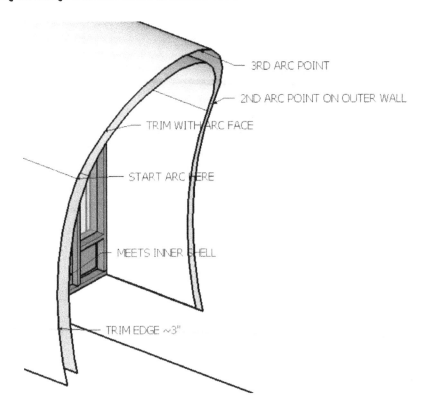

- 3RD ARC POINT
- 2ND ARC POINT ON OUTER WALL
- TRIM WITH ARC FACE
- START ARC HERE
- MEETS INNER SHELL
- TRIM EDGE ~3"

8. Windows

Before starting the windows, here is what you have accomplished. If you've made it this far you are doing very well. Still a lot to do.

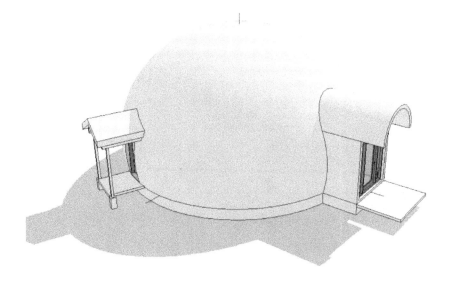

Now add four windows, all the same, one in each room ninety degrees apart. Start by adding four more lines to our Center Lines.

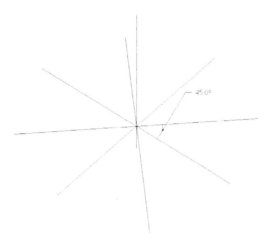

Here is an overview of the window object.

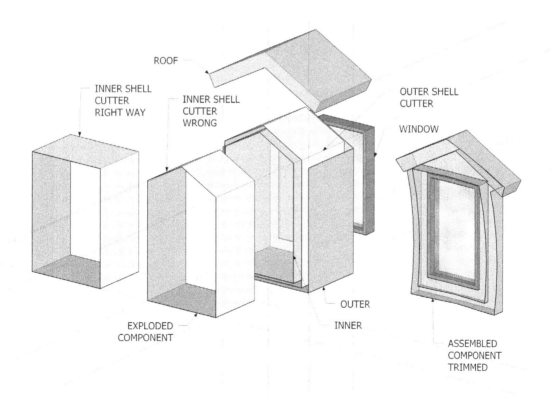

On the new Window layer make a box 5' x 6' x 3'6' on the horizontal plane and add a peak 16" high.

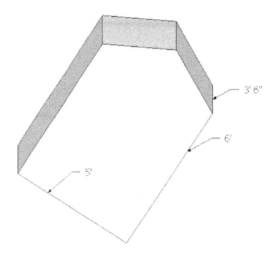

Make another box 6" smaller on the sides and bottom, but with the top still touching the sloped roof. Remove the roof.

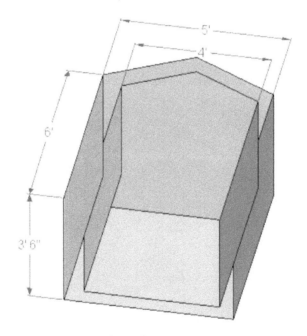

Drag/Copy a second set. Build a 3' x 5' window, make an opening for it and move it into position.

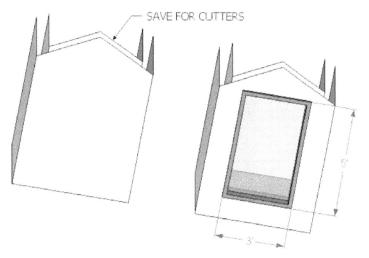

SAVE FOR CUTTERS

5'

3'

Add a roof to the inner box. Later we will discover this is a mistake. The roof should be horizontal on the inner box. Finding and correcting mistakes is part of the process. Select the inner box and place the parts on a new layer called Dome Cutter 2. Make a component called Cutter Shell Inner. Place the component on the new layer, too.

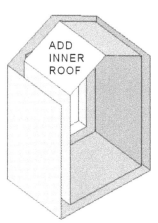

ADD INNER ROOF

Make a roof with a 6" overhang on the front and sides. You should have a group for the Window Box, the Window and the Window Roof. Rotate the window unit and the future cutters upright. Now select the window groups and make a component called Window. All of this is on the Window layer.

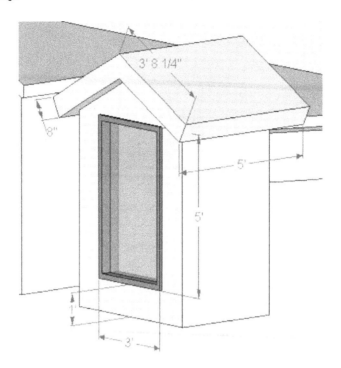

Make a cutter box component called Cutter Outer Shell, 3" smaller on both sides and the bottom, but the top 3" higher. Place it on the Dome Cutter layer. Position the component in the window unit between the inner and outer boxes. Place the component Cutter Shell Inner, created above, so it coincides with the inner box of the window unit.

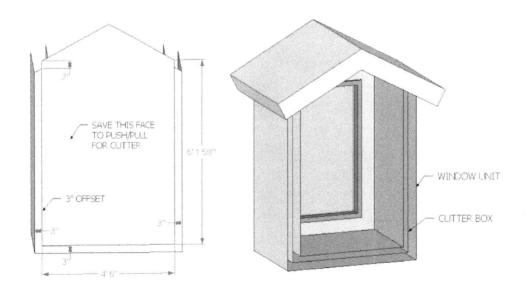

Move the window unit with the two cutters into position on the new 45 degree lines. The best way to do that accurately is to first position the window

50

centered at the back of the dome. Then turn off the Window layer, check to see if the Cutter Shell Outer component extends slightly outside of the outer shell at the equator. Adjust if necessary. To insure the Rotate tool is level, place a grouped 8' circle at the top of the vertical center line. Place the circle on a new layer called Center Circle. Make sure all three objects, the window unit and two cutters, are selected; now Rotate the window, roof and cutters 45 degrees. Then Rotate/Copy 90 degrees and created all four. Make the sill height 24".

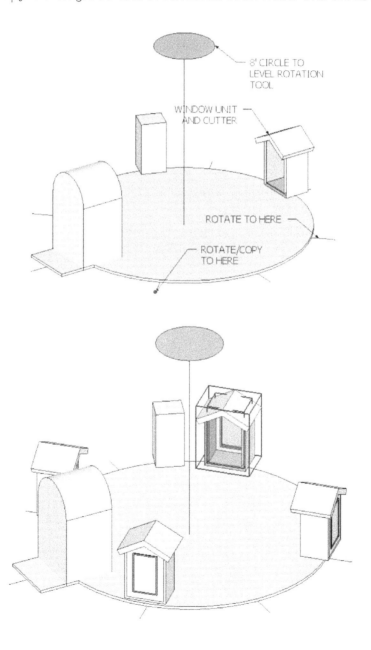

Turn off everything except the Outer Shell and Window layers. Edit and trim the Roof group with the Outer Shell. Notice all components are trimmed at once. Remove the unwanted roof parts. Use the Eraser tool to delete any extraneous lines on the under side of the roof.

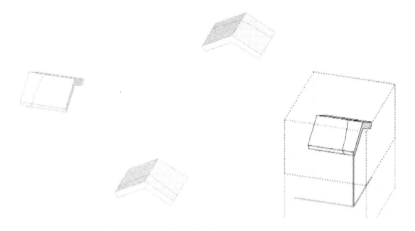

Turn off the Window layer; turn on the Dome Cutter layer. Trim the Outer shell. Turn off the Outer Shell and Dome Cutter layers. Trim just the two Window Box groups inside the Window component with the inner shell.

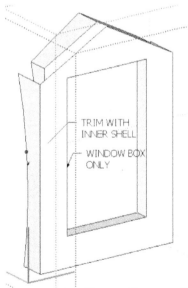

TRIM WITH
INNER SHELL

WINDOW BOX
ONLY

Turn off the Window layer. Turn on the Dome Cutter 2 and Inner Shell layers. Trim the inner shell with Cutter Shell Inner component. Turn off the Dome Cutter 2 layer.

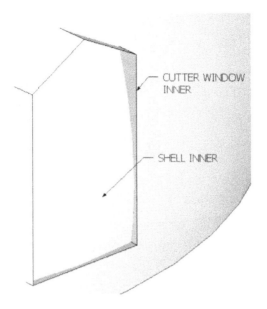

CUTTER WINDOW
INNER

SHELL INNER

Manually trim back the outer window box 3", putting that edge between the two dome shells.

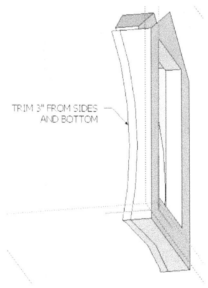

TRIM 3" FROM SIDES
AND BOTTOM

That should do it for the windows. Complicated, but one step at a time gets it done. Doing it takes much less time than reading about it. The hardest part is over.

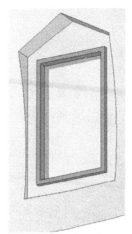

Inside view still showing incorrect ceiling.

9. Skylights

Another progress check is seen below. Looks nearly finished from the outside. Let's make a Scene. Rotate your model to match the view below. Turn on shadows. Adjust the sliders to find interesting settings. Open the Scene palette. Click the plus sign to create a new scene. Change the name from Scene "x" to Progress View. Now you can go back to this view at any time with these layers and shadows. You can make a scene called All Off with just the Center Lines on. Make others called Interior Only, Floor Plan, Front Elevation, etc., as you need them.

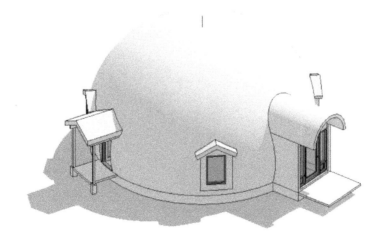

We will have two skylights. One for the top of the dome to give light, to take advantage of the chimney effect on warm days and to vent kitchen odors. Here are the objects needed.

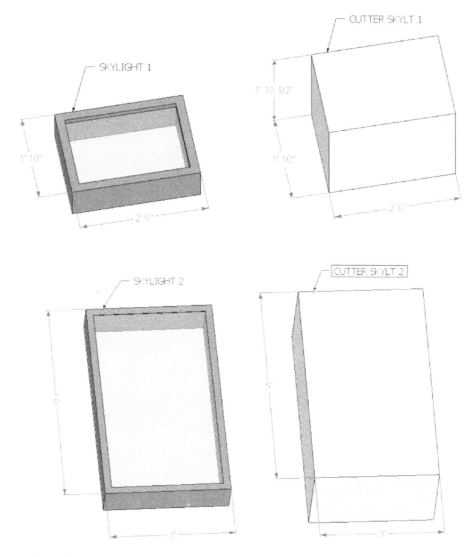

Position the skylight and its cutter together. Use the Section Plane tool to check the angle with the dome. Cut the skylight openings. Make the sill height on Skylight 2 about 2'-9".

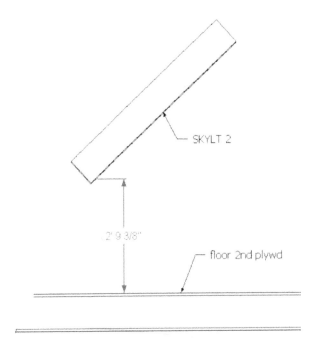

SKYLT 2

2' 9 3/8"

floor 2nd plywd

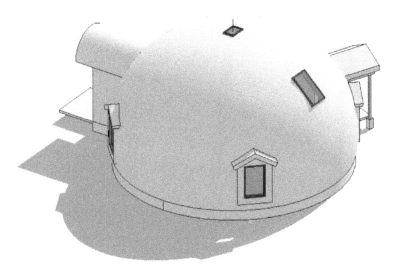

If you made it this far you have an attractive and accurate, neat and tidy model. Accuracy will be important when you start the working drawings.

10. Finish 2nd Floor

You need to add the guardrail, walls, doors for storage and settee to the second floor. The uprights will be similar to those on the stairs. Walls first...

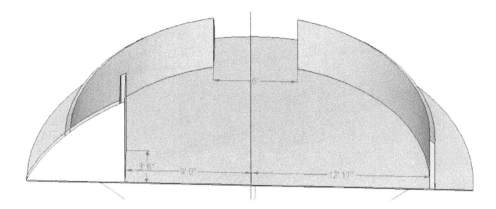

With a 16" high settee and storage doors the loft begins to shape up. Openings were not cut for the storage doors because you have to draw the line somewhere. The walls on the left will hide the hot water heater.

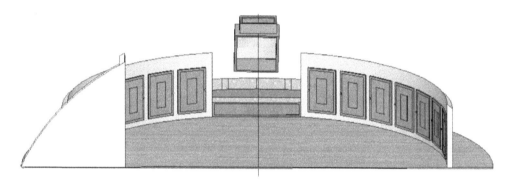

Time to build the guardrail. You can simply Drag/Copy the uprights and glass already modeled.

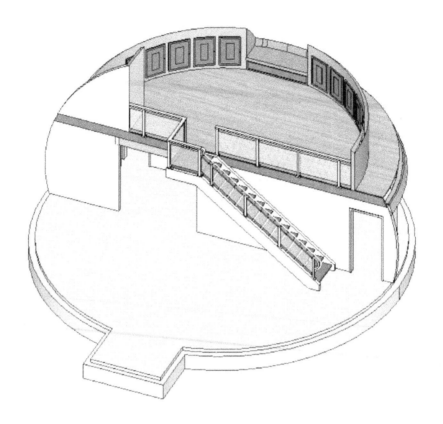

11. Kitchen, Bath, Bedroom

You want all the usual conveniences in the kitchen and bath. Let's start with the kitchen. The L shaped kitchen was found on 3D Warehouse. With a few modifications and the addition of the breakfast bar it will do. Some models on 3D Warehouse are more elaborate than needed for designing a house. If it goes over half a megabyte you might want to cancel the download and search for 'simple kitchen'. Or build your own and get just what you want. I need a wall space of 32+" for a refrigerator and may need to move that door to the bathroom. Normally the sink would be on the plumbing wall, but the kitchen seems to function better with the stove there instead.

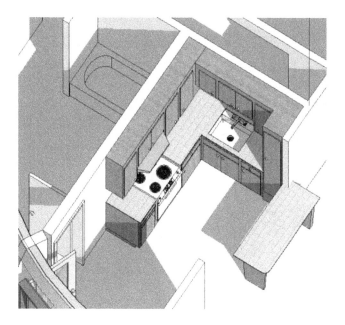

We will need to move that door to the bathroom. 2'-1" is available now and the door can be moved 9" for a total of 34".

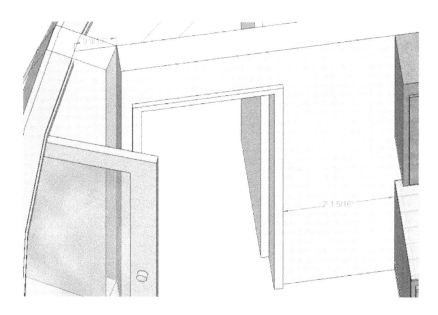

After extending the plumbing wall the refer fits. Now re-trim the short angled wall.

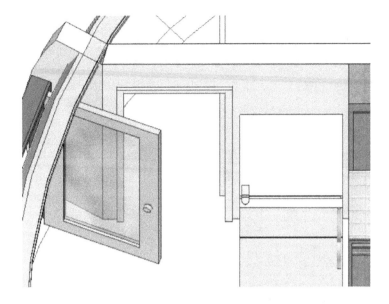

On the opposite wall add a washer/dryer vent less appliance. This will save a lot of space and mean one less dome penetration to deal with. A worktop has been added and storage cabinets above. You notice a problem. The upper right corner of the cabinet conflicts with the corbel. Building an accurate model has a big benefit. You can identify problem areas in the model rather than on the construction site. You can reduce the width or have the cabinet custom build to accommodate the corbel. Let's do the latter.

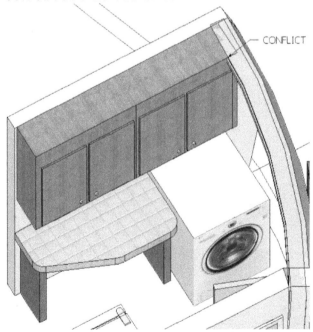

Notice the washer/dryer. I found a photo online of the actual machine and used it on a simple box rather than try to model all the detail.

The Bath is next. The tub, commode and vanity are from 3D Warehouse. Always check to see if downloads are actual real world sizes. The tub needed to be adjusted.

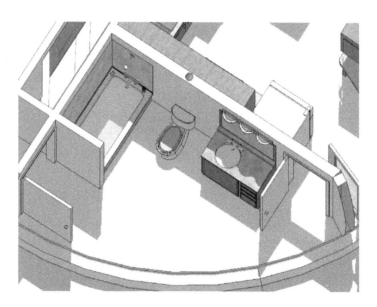

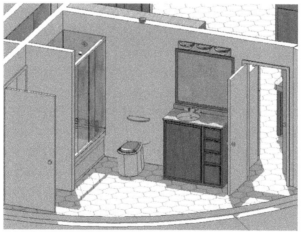

In the Bedroom I've added a linen closet by the Bath door. SketchUp reflections are hopefully in the future somewhere. This is a fake reflection with an image I added of the bed in the mirrored doors.

12. Furniture, Appliances, Etc.

Add furniture, a ceiling fan, stools, dining table and chairs, sofa, bed and woodstove. Many of these items found on 3D Warehouse required extensive modification or where modeled from scratch. When you do interior views plants, people and other things can be added.

Caution. Often people get carried away and put too much detail into an object for our purposes. We want very simple models with a small file size. In most cases you will be better off making the object yourself. When downloading models from 3D Warehouse you could open them on in a separate instance of SketchUp. Using the View > Face Style > X-ray, see if the model has unnecessary internal faces. All you need is the outside skin. Check the Layers palette. Did you inherit a lot of new layers with the model? If you still want to use it, delete all the internal modeling that won't show. Eliminate unnecessary groups and components. Place everything on Layer O and delete all the extra layers. Use the big minus sign in the Layers palette and choose the Move contents to Default layer option. If a part you want to keep has an excessive amount of faces, reduce them to the minimum needed to look ok. A common problem found in small curved or rounded details and in trees and plants. Now you can copy and paste into your SketchUp instance with the dome.

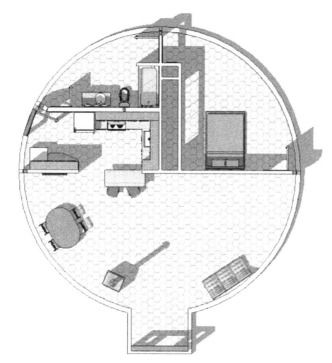

The first floor 3D plan view.

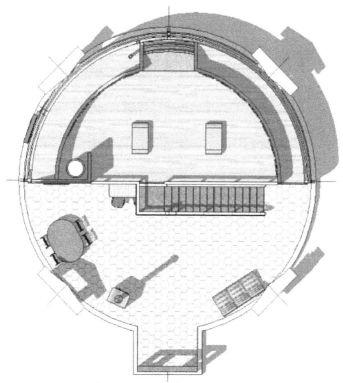

The second floor 3D plan.

13. Correcting Problems

As you build the model problems may be noticed that you might not catch with just a set of 2D plans. This is especially true for domes. You've already dealt with a couple of conflicts. Another issue was the head room from the stair landing to the ceiling fan from 3D Warehouse. At seven feet it was marginal. By shortening the shaft you gain 7". Might be a good idea to move it closer to the skylight as well. Make a note about this on the working drawings. It was eventually moved a bit further from the center and more over the stairs when the wood stove was moved.

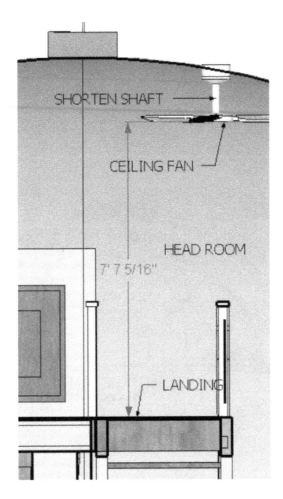

When making the four windows I should have noticed that the pitched ceiling design conflicted with the corbel.

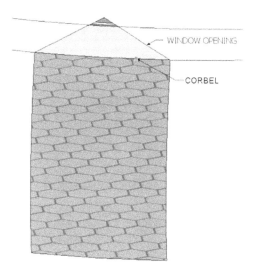

It can be fixed by deleting the pitched roof from the inner window box and adding a horizontal ceiling.

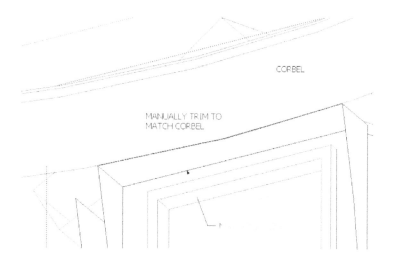

To patch the inner shell you can make a copy of the shell, the Center Lines and one of the Cutter Win Inner objects. Be sure to make the shell unique or you will cut the original shell, too. Rotate the copied cutter 45 degrees to a blank spot on the shell. Edit the shell by Intersect Faces > With Model. Drag/Copy the triangle to the original shell; rotate into position in one of the openings. Rotate copies for the other three. Delete the extra copies.

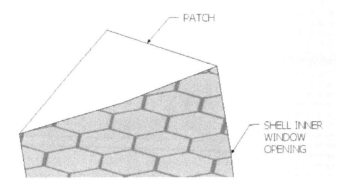

This won't show on the exterior. It will show on the windows in the living and dining rooms. The only way to fix that is to start with a new inner shell and re-cut all the openings. Since you have all the dome cutters made and in place it would not be too hard to do after fixing the window cutter. I will leave it for now.

14. Heating/Cooling

This dome is being planned for Willcox, Arizona. The heating requirements are minimal. Add 3' electric baseboard heaters in each room. For cooling add a thru-the-wall air conditioning unit.

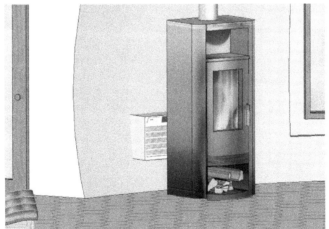

A/C installed in the dome behind the wood stove.

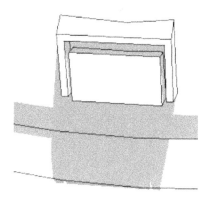

A protective surround is placed over the air conditioner on the exterior custom fabricated from ¼" steel plate bolted to the dome. Ask the contractor to submit a shop drawing for approval.

The ceiling fan will help with both heating and cooling. The center skylight has a remote control. It can be opened on cool evenings to dissipate the heat of the day if conditions are right.

A hole must be made in the dome for the woodstove and for the plumbing vent. The dome constructor will need to know exactly the location of these openings, as well as all the others. First make a cricket for each pipe to protect it from the elements. Start with a rectangle 18" x 60".

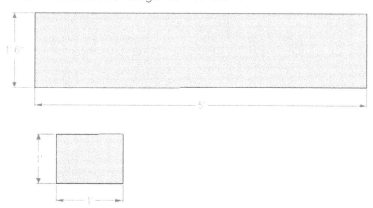

And a 12" square.

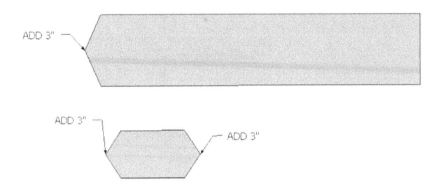

Add triangular extensions as shown.

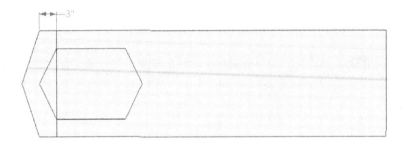

Group the smaller shape and position as shown.

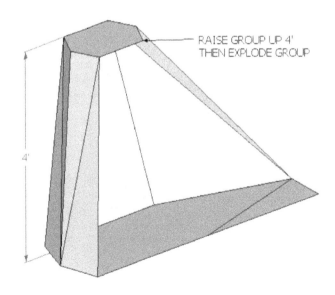

Move smaller shape up 4'. Add edges as shown.

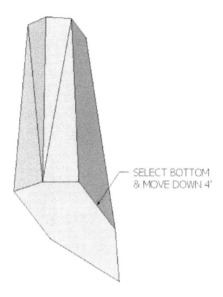

It appears to need scaling vertically. Select the bottom face and Move down 4'.

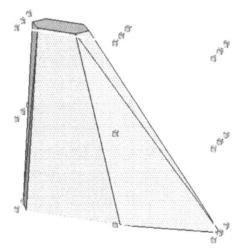

Scale the pointed side making it longer, about 1.5.

SOFTEN EDGES
~65 DEGREES

Group and call it Cricket 1. Place it on a new layer called Crickets. Soften the edges ~65 degrees. Rotate/Copy the cricket and scale it for the plumbing vent pipe. In the end the wood stove was moved near the stairs and its cricket was eliminated.

15. Electrical

Now move the ceiling fan to the Electrical layer along with the air conditioner. Make a simple 3D object for the baseboard heaters. Be sure to make the Electrical 3D layer active. Make a component and place it on the same layer. Put one under each window, later changed to two, and one under the counter in the laundry area.

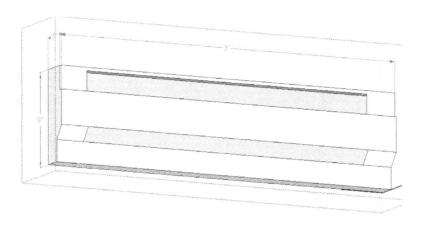

Here you see it in place under a window.

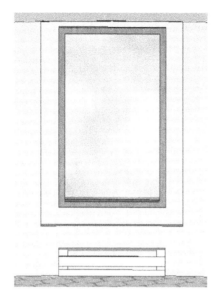

The electrical panel can not be just an after thought. You will need 30" of clear wall space minimum and a minimum of 36" clear in front of it. It must be easily accessible in case the electricity needs to be turned off in a hurry. You only have two places available that meet the requirements. Under the stairs and at the head of the stairs. Take the second one.

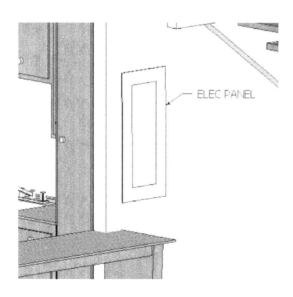

ELEC PANEL

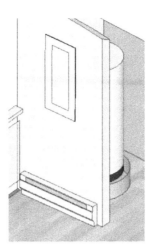

Show all the smoke detectors, outlets, light switches and light fixtures on the 2D plans. Modeling them in 3D is optional.

16. Plumbing

You already have most of the plumbing items: bath tub, lavatory, commode, kitchen sink, washer/dryer and hot water heater. The most important thing is the location of the vent stack. Let's make a cylinder and cut a hole in both shells. A good time to do the double-walled stove pipe, too. Put these cylinders on a new layer called Dome Cutters 3.

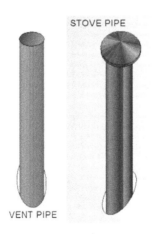

Plumbing fixtures and appliances. Note the vent pipe over the w/c.

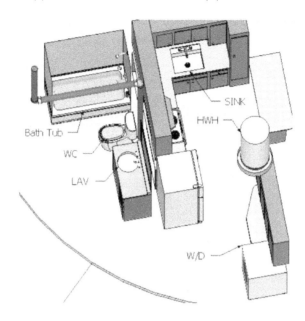

Step 2: Visualization

Exterior View

The model is done. More an aid for the design process, not part of the working drawings, let's do an exterior and an interior rendering. SketchUp renderings are not photorealistic, but they are useful. Add landscaping and people and do a little post processing and they look pretty good.

Image as exported from the program.

After post-processing in Paint Shop Pro.

The only limit is time and imagination. For the background I used a photo taken on the California coast to which I applied a Silk Screen filter. A nice photo with a grassy lawn was used for the yard. Noise was added to the dome for an interesting texture. Values and colors were adjusted. Finally, the lady of the house was added. Now one that looks more like Arizona.

As exported from SketchUp.

Enhanced in Paint Shop Pro.

Interior View

For the interior rendering the camera was set at a sixty degree angle of view. Two plants and a figure were downloaded from 3D Warehouse. Two renderings were exported.

Image with shadows on.

Second image without shadows.

Overlaid images.

Over-laying these two images in Paint Shop Pro and blending with Lighter setting produces the image above. Color, gradation and texture were added to the dome wall. Color was added to the tiles. The triangles over the windows were brushed out. The segments on the arch to the entry have become a smooth curve. All openings have been rounded. The pink area around the far window was darkened as were the baseboard heater and the semi-circle above the entry door. You may see other changes as well.

77

Step 3: The Airform

If there is something unusual about your design you will have contacted Monolithic, Inc. in Italy, Texas prior to beginning the model to be certain no problems will arise with the airform. It is possible to model a dome in SketchUp that can't be inflated.

"Monolithic's construction process requires an Airform. It's an integral part of every Monolithic Dome, Monolithic Cabin, EcoShell and Crenosphere. The Monolithic Airform is a balloon-like, inflatable structure that determines the shape and size of a dome. It's made of PVC-coated nylon or polyester fabric, available in several weights and a rainbow of colors. Each Monolithic Airform is designed for a specific project and manufactured in Bruco, our 240' × 60' factory equipped with state-of-the-art machinery." From monolithic.com.

By the end of Step 2 you should be certain that no more changes will be made to the dome itself. Openings may move or be fine tuned, but the size and shape will stay the same. When ordering the airform send the opening/dome section drawing sheet to Monolithic. The dome constructor may want to order the airform himself.

Unfold a gore. If you want to make your own airform, SketchUp can be used to determine the size and shape of the gores. Use the Follow Me tool to make at least a partial outer dome shell. You will only need one gore. Explode if necessary and Drag/Copy one of the forty-eight gores. With the Unfold tool select the lowest face of the gore, select the next adjacent face. The first face will rotate in line with the second. Select the face third from the bottom and so forth until the entire gore is unfolded into a straight line. Rotate the straightened gore parallel with the XY plane. The example below is one of 48. It may be more practical to use 24 gores.

2' 3 1/2"   2' 4 1/4"

29' 10 1/4"

Step 4: Plan Review

Working drawings, also called construction documents and plans, are part of your agreement with the general contractor or with the subs if you are acting as the construction manager. In that sense they are a legal document. You will want to take great care in their preparation.

Permit Packet

One of the first things to do is ask for a copy of local requirements from the plan review office. Each will have its unique items as well as the usual drawings. Getting a permit will mean providing everything listed. This is not the time to stand your ground and argue over minor issues. Far better to be agreeable, friendly and accommodating. Treat the plan reviewer as an important part of your construction team. Be thankful for any deficiencies in your drawings brought to your attention. Don't be defensive. If you feel your opinion should prevail, be polite, courteous and document your position. The appeals process or law suit is strictly a last resort. It might be easier to build in a different location in a different jurisdiction.

For our purposes here, the project will be located in Willcox, Arizona. A copy of the Cochise County Residential Permit Packet has been provided. The Intake Checklist has several items related to working drawings:

Complete site plan, see Site Plan Instructions

If new residence, a lighting plan and lighting worksheet.

Three sets of construction plans.

Construction plan checklist, completed.

Truss calculations, two sets, not for domes.

The next page is Residential Site Plan Instructions. It suggests drawing on 8 ½" x 11" paper. I recently submitted the site plan on a set of working drawings, which is not unusual. It passed inspection. You could do both just to be sure. The septic system is already in the ground, so you don't need to have a certified Septic System Site Evaluator prepare the site plan.

Residential Site Plan Instructions

Draw site plan on 8½" x 11" paper. For all items, note whether existing (e) or proposed (p). NOTE: The site plan must be complete and clearly legible.

If a new septic system is proposed, the site plan must be prepared by a Health Department certified Septic System Site Evaluator. Contact the Community Development Department, Planning, Zoning & Building Safety at (520) 432-9240 if you have questions or need assistance with your application.

Required for all residential permit applications

1. Tax parcel ID number, north arrow and scale (if a scale is used)
2. Property lines and all dimensions (from Assessors' Parcel map) – include entire parcel
3. If parcel is a new split, show parent parcel and your parcel's location – with dimensions
4. All easements – label type (road right of way, utility, drainage, etc.) and width
5. Location of utility lines (electric, gas, water, etc.)
6. Roads adjoining the property: name of road, surface material, distance from property line to edge of actual road
7. Driveways: location, surface material, distance to closest property line
8. Show direction of drainage on the property
9. Any construction related to a wash, such as a bridge, culvert, dip crossing, or fill, either on the parcel or off-site. Note whether temporary or permanent.
10. Location, depth, and width of all drainageways or washes larger than 3 feet deep or 5 feet wide (include washes located on adjacent properties within 300 feet of project)
11. Distance from proposed structures to any drainageway or wash
12. Distance from structures to all property lines and roads, and distance between residences on the subject parcel
13. Location of wells, septic tanks, leach fields and 100% expansion areas, and distance from septic system to buildings, property lines, any drainageway or wash, & locations of test pits
14. Direction of slope of land in area of proposed leach fields and expansion areas, indicate % slope
15. Location, dimensions and height of all buildings, and their uses
16. Location, height, length and material of walls and fences – for chainlink fences, note if slatted

Required if applicable to your project

17. If outdoor lighting is proposed, location, fixture type (such as 18 watt fluorescent, 75 watt incandescent, 250 watt low pressure sodium, etc.), shielding, and height of fixture
18. If a new residence, a completed Lighting Worksheet is required
19. If a mobile or manufactured home, show location and type of all accessories such as decks, awnings, skirting, etc. Construction plans and State approval are required if accessories are part of the original sales contract
20. If a solid fence or wall is proposed, distance from road surface (travelway) of all adjoining roads, speed limit of road (if posted) and distance to driveways on neighboring parcels within 20 feet of proposed wall
21. If barn or shed is proposed, note if for animals, storage, or other use
22. If a pool is proposed, pool size, location, setbacks to property lines; pool enclosure location, type, height. Type of pool cover? Required by 1820.01A of zoning regulations.
23. If clearing (removing vegetation by scraping the land) more than 1 acre, show dimensions of area to be cleared, and proposed dust and erosion control measures
24. If new SFR (site built only) on construction plans show the "Gray Water Plumbing" and "Hot Water on Demand" as required per Sierra Vista Sub-watershed Water Conservation Overlay Zone
25. If new or replacement "Outdoor Sprinkler System" or "Evaporative Coolers" show compliance with Sierra Vista Sub-watershed Water Conservation Overlay Zone
26. If a Solar Panel is proposed, installed only by a Licensed Contractor.
27. If a Wind Turbine is proposed, site plan required for roof mounted, disclosure statement required

The example site plan provided in the packet is here:

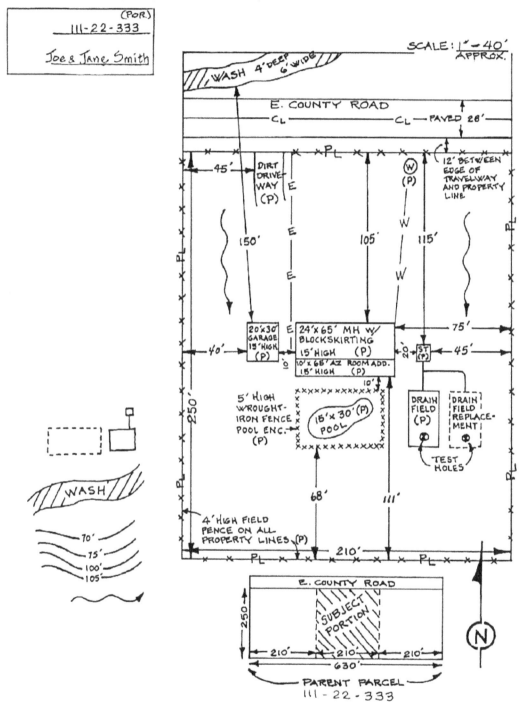

111

Real Working Drawings

And the Sample Light Plan from the packet:

SAMPLE LIGHTING PLAN

RESIDENTIAL LIGHTING WORKSHEET

Fixture ID on Plans	Fixture Type and Wattage	No. of Fixtures	Height above Ground¹	Lumens per Fixture	Total Lumens for Fixture Type
Existing					
None					
Subtotal					
Proposed					
A	60 W. Incandescent	2		890	1780
B	18 W. Compact Flour.	1		1200	1200
C	(2) 75 W. PAR	3		1400	4200
D	75 W. Halogen	2		700	1400
Subtotal					8580
Grand Total					8580

Total Lumens 8580 Total project acreage (developed area) 1 acre
Lumens per acre permitted: 20,000
Lumens per acre proposed: 8580
Are all proposed fixtures fully shielded? No
If no, identify which fixtures and exemption type A - less than 1000 lumens
Notes: C to be aimed half way between straight down and horizontal (45°)

¹ If pole mounted

Type A	Type B	Type C	Type D

82

LAMP DATA

Lamp Wattage	Initial Lumens
Incandescent	
25 W	150
40 W	460
60 W	890
75W	1210
100 W	1750
150 W	2880
300 W	6360
1000 W	23800
Compact Fluorescent	
5 W	250
7 W	400
13 W	900
18 W	1200
26 W	1800
32 W	2900
Tungsten-Halogen	
250 W	4700
500 W	10700
1000 W	19000
1500 W	36000
Mercury Vapor	
100 W	4000
175 W	8500
400 W	23000
700 W	44000
1000 W	61000

Lamp Wattage	Initial Lumens
Metal Halide	
175 W	14000
250 W	20000
400 W	40000
1000 W	115000
PAR (Parabolic Aluminized Floods & Spots)	
150 W	1740
HPS (High Pressure Sodium)	
50 W	3300
70 W	5800
100 W	9500
150 W	16000
200 W	22000
250 W	30000
310 W	37000
400 W	50000
1000 W	140000
LPS (Low Pressure Sodium)	
18 W	1800
35 W	4800
55 W	8000
90 W	13500
135 W	22500
180 W	33000

Fluorescent (Standard Cool-White, 1.5-inch tubes)	
21 W	1190
30 W	2050
36 W	2450
39 W	3000
50 W	3700
52 W	3900
55 W	4600
70 W	5400
75 W	6300

The values on this Lamp Data sheet are to be used unless other verified lumen values are submitted.

Here is a handy checklist of items you must have on our sheets to be turned in completed with the plans.

Residential Submittal Requirements:

Based on the 2003 International Residential Code.

(To be completed by applicant)

Submittal Documents
- ☐ Three Sets of Construction Documents. Minimum preferred size 24"x36". (1/4" Scale Recommended.)
- ☐ Two *Sealed* copies of Truss Calculations, or deferred note on drawings.
- ☐ One copy of the Sierra Vista Sub-Watershed document signed and dated. (If applicable)
- ☐ One copy of the Cochise County Lighting worksheet if not shown on plans.

Foundation Plan
- ☐ Show plan view of complete dimensioned foundation layout.
- ☐ Provide details of footing type, size, and reinforcements.
- ☐ Sealed calculations and plans for engineered slabs. (Post tension, raft, etc.)
- ☐ Location and type of anchors and hold-downs.
- ☐ Concrete compressive strength.
- ☐ Minimum soil bearing pressure.
- ☐ 95% Minimum soil compaction

Roof/Framing Plan
- ☐ Plan view of structural components: beams, trusses, headers, and structural connection details.
- ☐ Size, spacing, species, and grade of materials.
- ☐ All details referenced on Roof or Framing Plan.
- ☐ Roof slopes, drainage, scuppers, and skylights.

Plumbing Plan
- ☐ Show location and material of all piping, drainage waste, vent, and water piping with developed length.
- ☐ Show location and developed length of gas piping with appliance demands.
- ☐ Provide water and fixture unit tables. (For sizing purposes and Health Department review)

Floor Plan
- ☐ Show proposed construction.
- ☐ Show complete dimensions, window and door callouts, and label all room uses.
- ☐ Show braced wall panel locations per Section R 602.10 Wall Bracing.
- ☐ Indicate separation between garage and dwelling. (5/8" Type X per amendment)
- ☐ Show all cabinets and fixture locations.
- ☐ Show all safety glazing at hazardous locations.

Exterior Elevations/Building Sections
- ☐ Show all sides of the structure, window sill heights, exterior finishes, chimney heights, top of wall and roof heights.
- ☐ Show cross section of structure with room labels, interior finishes callouts, ceiling and drop heights.
- ☐ Cross reference to framing and foundation sections.
- ☐ Roof Ventilation calculations. Identify type and location.

Mechanical Plan
- ☐ Show room uses.
- ☐ Indicate heating and cooling units, type, location.
- ☐ Show fuel burning appliances combustion air.
- ☐ Show supply and return air routes.
- ☐ Show diffuser (register) locations.
- ☐ Shows exhaust fan locations.

Electrical Plan
- ☐ Show room uses.
- ☐ Plan view showing panel location, receptacles, lights, circuits, ground fault interrupters, arc fault interrupters, and smoke alarms.
- ☐ Panel schedule showing circuits.
- ☐ Service entrance diagram. (Riser diagram).
- ☐ Load calculations and service size.
- ☐ Show compliance with the Cochise County Light Pollution Ordinance. (May be completed by worksheet.)

Building Code

The plan reviewer's bible is the building code. You should really have a copy of it, all 868 pages. The International Residential Code, IRC, for One-and-Two Family Dwellings is available on the internet for around $75 in paperback. Wouldn't it be nice to have an online, searchable copy for free? Yes, it would and you can find it here: http://bulk.resource.org/codes.gov/bsc.ca.gov/gov.ca.bsc.2010.02.5.html

Want to know all the code says about stairs? Click Ctrl+f and type in Stair. Click down through the document. You'll learn about lighting requirements for stairs, how close glazing can be, what head clearance is required, as well as the mandated size of treads and risers and the height of handrails. You may not be building in California, but probably most of the requirements are the same as in your area.

Step 5: Sheets, Title blocks & Borders

There is not a sheet size requirement given here. The usual sheet size is 24' x 36" and you should use that size unless you have a good reason not to. Check to be certain. In this case 18" x 24" will be used so that when reproduced on these pages they will be more legible.

Sheets & Border

The SketchUp sheets will be sized so that the floor plans are at quarter inch scale. That means 1/4" = 1 foot. At quarter inch scale a 36' diameter circle would be 36 divided by four or 9". Conversely, an 18" x 24" sheet would be 18x4 by 24x4 or 72' x 96'. For 24" x 36" sheets are 96' x 144'. You'll want a half inch margin all round...1/2" x 4' = 2'. Draw the border and title block first, 68' x 92', and then the edge of the paper, 72' x 96'.

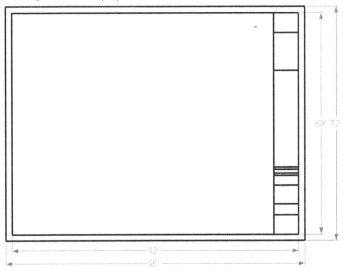

Make a component called Border Title Block. It can be left on Layer 0.

Title Block

Now Edit Component. The title block can be about 2" (8') wide. Leave the text for the CAD program. Layout twelve sheets a safe distance from your model, ten shown here.

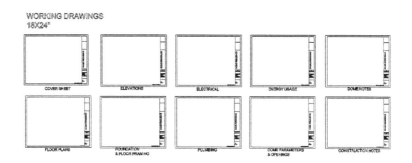

WORKING DRAWINGS
18X24"

COVER SHEET | ELEVATIONS | ELECTRICAL | ENERGY USAGE | DOME NOTES

FLOOR PLANS | FOUNDATION & FLOOR FRAMING | PLUMBING | DOME PARAMETERS & OPENINGS | CONSTRUCTION NOTES

Sheet Names

A-1 COVER
A-2 FLOOR PLANS
A-3 ELEVATIONS
A-4 RINGBEAM & FRAMING
A-5 ELECTRICAL
A-6 LOAD CALCULATIONS
A-7 PLUMBING & SECTIONS
A-8 DOME OPENINGS
A-9 ENERGY USAGE
A-10 CONSTRUCTION NOTES
A-11 DOME NOTES
A-12 SITE PLAN & STAIR DETAIL

More sheets can be added if needed.

Step 6: 3D to 2D

2D Drawings & Images

Using one of five methods extract these 2D drawings from the model for the layouts:

> First floor plan
>
> Second floor plan
>
> Exterior view
>
> Four elevations
>
> Ringbeam plan
>
> Framing plan
>
> Two building sections
>
> Dome openings top
>
> Dome openings 4 elevations
>
> Dome only section
>
> Dome wall/ringbeam detail —
>
> Main entry/footing study
>
> Window/eyebrow study
>
> Corbel detail
>
> Site plan
>
> Stair detail

Method 1: Face Section

1. With the model setup for a first floor plan, show only built-in items like walls, cabinets and stairs, plus major appliances. Don't show moveable items like furniture. Also show the Center Lines layer.

2. Create a 50' x 50' horizontal face in a group. Put the new face near the bottom of the windows, just above the sill so some glass will show. Edit Group > Select face > Right click > Intersect faces > With model.

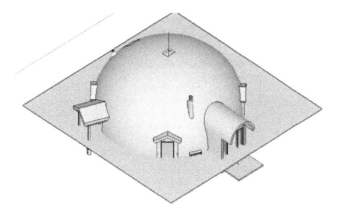

Close the group and move it to one side.

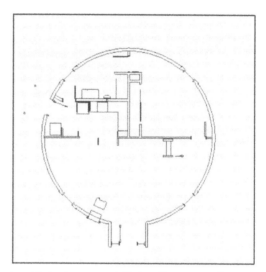

3. Lower the group on the XY plane and Edit Group > Delete all the faces and the four lines of the border. For the first floor plan this method is better. It is precise and fast. You can quickly add missing lines and objects with SketchUp tools.

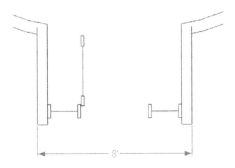

Method 1 is precisely accurate and fast.

Method 2: Jpg Image

Let's do an exterior elevation using another method.

A. In Parallel Projection mode, select front view with Engineering Style, Hidden Line, Edges and Profiles on. Zoom to fill the screen. Adjust the SketchUp window sideways if needed. Leave a small space around the image. Then, File > Export > 2D Graphic... > Options... > Best quality and longer side at 2400 pixels. Assuming the image on the final printed sheet will be about 8" this will give 300 ppi. Click Export.

B. When you bring the image into DraftSight...

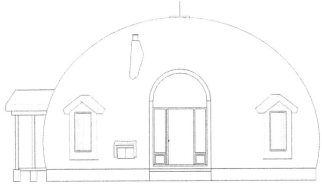

Insert > Reference image.... Scale to the approximate correct size. A scale factor of 512 worked for my images. Measure a known length, calculate the scale factor for correction and scale again. For my layout the images were scaled down from full size to fit the sheet.

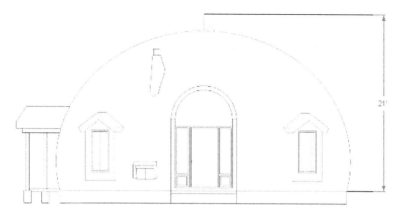

Image after scaling.

C. Optional. Using in SketchUp or the CAD program manually trace over the image to make the elevation a vector drawing. Delete the image.

Method 2 is fast and accurate enough for many uses. No point in putting images into the SketchUp layout because they will not get saved in the .dxf file. You will bring them in and scale them in DraftSight. For now in SketchUp you can put a rectangle on the proper sheet and label it to show you have made the image. All of the illustrations in this book were done in a similar way.

Method 3: Jpg to Dxf

Set SketchUp for Engineering Style, Top view and Parallel Projection. For the first floor plan position a Section Plane just above the window sill in the glass area facing downward... Zoom to fill the working area with the model. Leave a small white space around the model. Resize the window sideways if needed.

1. Go to File > Export > 2D graphic... > Export Type > .jpg > Options... > 7200 pixels in longer side > Best quality. Call it 1ST_FLOOR_PLAN_SU_JPG and save in a new folder called Layout Drawings.

2. Open the free version of Wintopo, the raster to vector conversion software. Find it at WinTopo.com. Open the file from Step 1. Go to Image > Contrast... > 255 > Ok. Move the slider all the way to the right. Now click the One-touch Vectorization button. When the process finishes go to View > click to uncheck Show Raster Image. Zoom in and inspect the lines. Click on the Save Vector As button. Save as an AutoCAD dxf file called 1ST_FLOOR_PLAN_WT_DXF.

3. Open the file from Step 2 in DraftSight, the free 2D CAD software. Go to View > Zoom > Fit. You will need to resize it. Find a line with a known length. You can use the horizontal center line which you know to be 40'. That measures 452'-6". Divide 40 by 452.5 = .0884. Select the entire drawing. Click the Scale button on the right toolbar. Enter .0884 in the Command Window and press Enter. Check that the horizontal center line measures 40'. If all is well, File > Save As > Save As Type > R14 ASCII Drawing (*.dxf) > File Name > 1ST_FLOOR_PLAN_DS-R14_DXF > Save.

4. In a second instance of SketchUp open a new file with Engineering Style, Top view, Parallel Projection. Go to File > Import DXF > import the file from Step 3. Use these settings: Help options: None; Import units: Inches; Select origin: by Pointer; Polylines: to Edges; and Materials: None. Copy and paste this drawing into your other SketchUp instance with the layout sheets.
To see the Import DXF on the File menu you will need to download and install the plugin called my_dxf_In_v1.22.rb in the Plugins folder of Google SketchUp. It can be found by doing a Google search. SketchUcation Community Forum should be the first result.

This whole process takes only a few minutes, much less time than to read and comprehend the directions. The end product is well worth the effort...a pretty good vector drawing you can't get any other way. You should have a very clean if slightly inaccurate vector drawing. My converted drawing is accurate at the mid-point of the two parallel lines, but 1/16" off at the corners. That is because WinTopo tends to miter corners just slightly or, as in this case, it made the right line is not quite vertical. For many purposes this would make no difference. Most house builders are happy to get within 1/4".

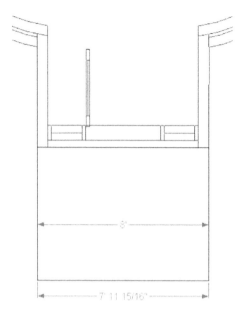

Method 3 takes a while and will never be 100% accurate, about 99.9% in this case. It might be good for very complicated drawings and perspective views, for example.

Method 4: Flatten to Plane

This method is all in SketchUp with the use of two plugins. You will need FlattenToPlane.rb and WorkPlane.rb made available for free at Sketchucation.com by TIG. I have made a Paypal donation and you may want to as well.

1. Set up your model with just the essentials for the first floor plan as before. I left the windows out because it will be easier to draw them in latter than to remove all the extra lines.

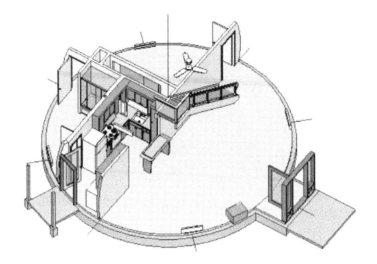

2. Make a 50' x 50' Workplane and position it below the model a ways. It doesn't need to be directly below the model, nor large enough to cover it.

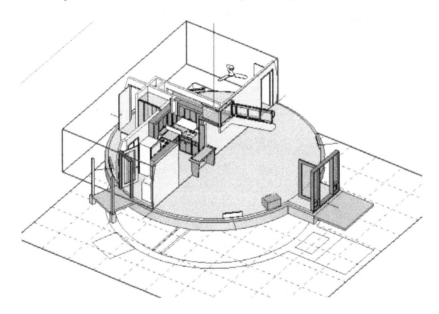

3. Select the group or component you want to flatten to the plane and select the Workplane. Here the Ringbeam and two concrete Pads have been flattened already. With the walls and Workplane selected, go to Plugins > Flatten to Plane. Expect to wait several minutes or more. Don't try to flatten too much at once because the program will freeze up. For the laundry wall cabinets I drew a face on top and flattened that. I did the same for the kitchen counter, cabinets, stove and sink, saving a lot of computing time and clean up. With more complicated geometry parts might be thrown out a hundred yards or so. They must then be repositioned or deleted.

Method 4 is precise, but slow. It took longer than Method 3, but it may still have its uses.

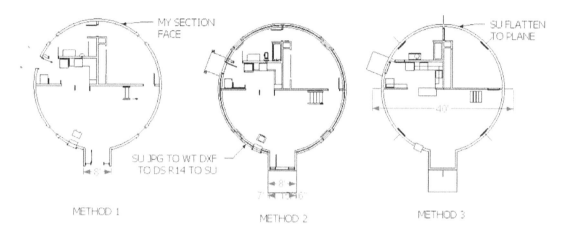

Method 5: SU Pro Trial

1. Create Scenes for all the 2D drawings you want to take from the model.

2. Download SketchUp Pro trial version. You will be able to use it, including LayOut, for 8 hours. LayOut is intended for creating multi-page presentation documents, but it can be used for construction documents. Eight hours is probably not enough time to do a full set of working drawings. From Layout you will be able to export 2D drawings of the model in .dxf or .dwg for import into a CAD program. For that 8 hours should be enough.

Step 7: The Preliminary Layout

It will take twelve sheets of 18" x 24" paper for the set of working drawings. At this preliminary stage you have some vector drawings and some shaded rectangles. The rectangles represent files you will bring in and assemble by the reference method in DraftSight. These files include .dxf, .jpg, .doc and possibly others. These sheets will be exported together without the text to a .dxf file which will then be opened in DraftSight for further drafting, dimensioning and adding of text. Below are the sheets as they are sent to DraftSight.

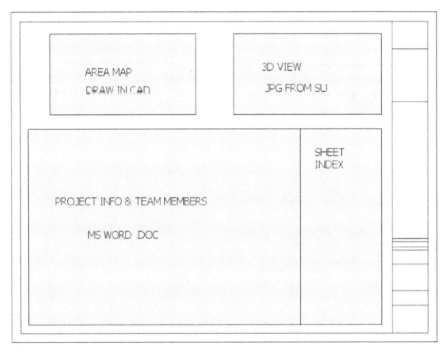

A-1 COVER

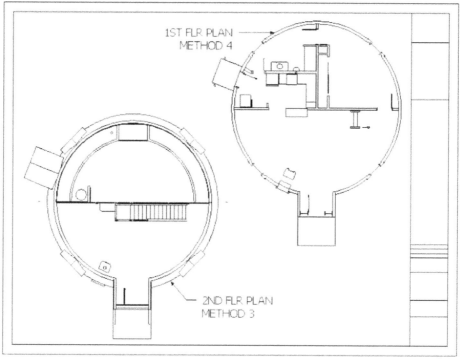

1ST FLR PLAN
METHOD 4

2ND FLR PLAN
METHOD 3

A-2 FLOOR PLANS

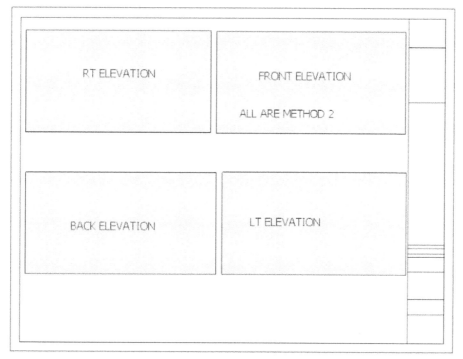

RT ELEVATION

FRONT ELEVATION

ALL ARE METHOD 2

BACK ELEVATION

LT ELEVATION

A-3 ELEVATIONS

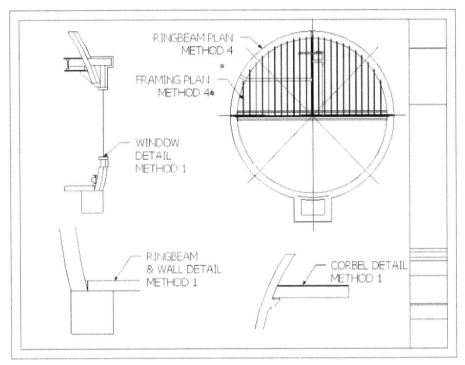

RINGBEAM PLAN
METHOD 4

FRAMING PLAN
METHOD 4

WINDOW
DETAIL
METHOD 1

RINGBEAM
& WALL DETAIL
METHOD 1

CORBEL DETAIL
METHOD 1

A-4 RINGBEAM/FRAMING

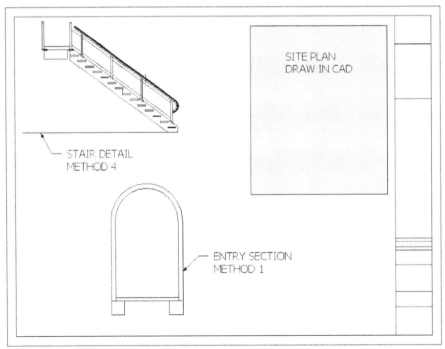

SITE PLAN
DRAW IN CAD

STAIR DETAIL
METHOD 4

ENTRY SECTION
METHOD 1

A-5 SITE PLAN, STAIRS, ENTRY

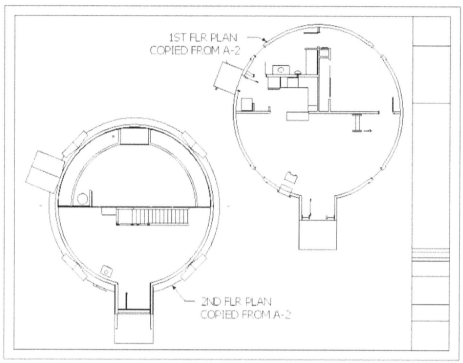

1ST FLR PLAN
COPIED FROM A-2

2ND FLR PLAN
COPIED FROM A-2

A-6 ELECTRICAL

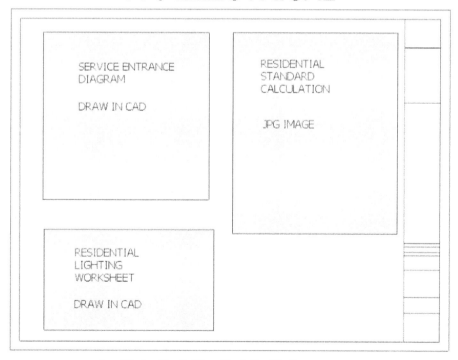

SERVICE ENTRANCE
DIAGRAM

DRAW IN CAD

RESIDENTIAL
STANDARD
CALCULATION

JPG IMAGE

RESIDENTIAL
LIGHTING
WORKSHEET

DRAW IN CAD

A-7 LOAD CALCS

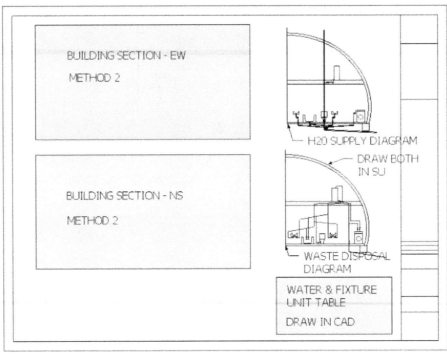

BUILDING SECTION - EW

METHOD 2

BUILDING SECTION - NS

METHOD 2

H20 SUPPLY DIAGRAM

DRAW BOTH
IN SU

WASTE DISPOSAL
DIAGRAM

WATER & FIXTURE
UNIT TABLE

DRAW IN CAD

A-8 PLUMBING

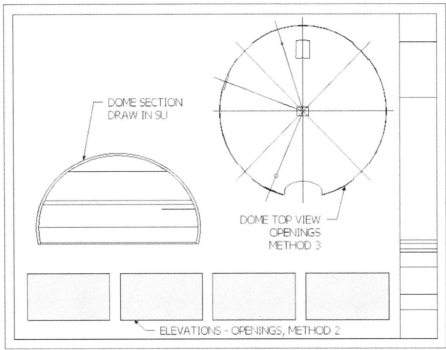

DOME SECTION
DRAW IN SU

DOME TOP VIEW
OPENINGS
METHOD 3

ELEVATIONS - OPENINGS, METHOD 2

A-9 DOME OPENINGS & SECTION

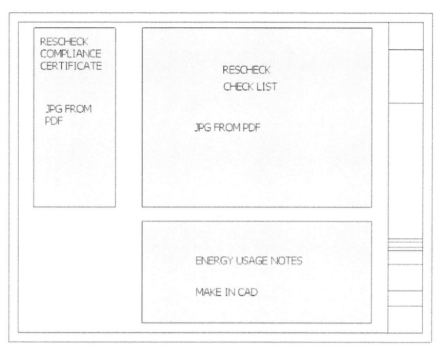

A-10 ENERGY USAGE

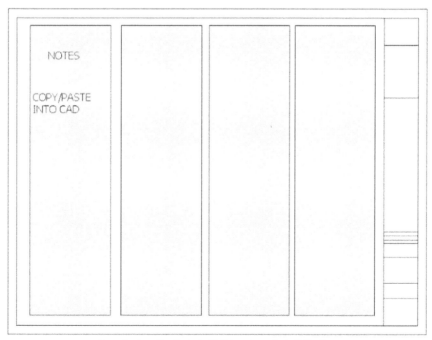

A-11 CONST. NOTES

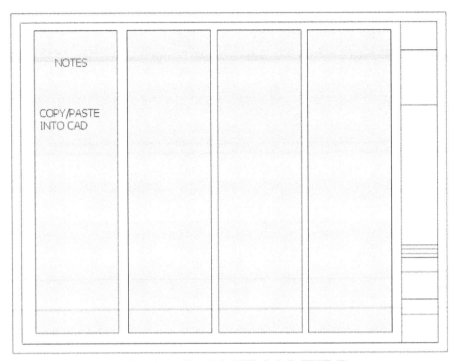

A-12 DOME NOTES

Step 8: The Finished Layout

There are several 2D CAD programs that can import 3D SketchUp files (.skp) including the Scenes. They are called 2.5D. Others can open 3D .dxf files. But none of them seem able to easily and smoothly make use of the model in layouts. At this writing the best approach is to extract 2D drawings from the model in SketchUp. Then save this as a .dxf file, open it in a CAD program and add the final drafting, text and dimension.

SketchUp to DraftSight

Note that when Exporting dxf from SketchUp you must be sure the file extension isn't accidentally deleted. If you try to open the file in a CAD program, but it doesn't show up in the folder, use Windows Explorer to make sure the file extension is there. It should look something like: layoutfromsetchup.dxf. If not, add the .dxf and it will then open in DraftSight.

Below is the DraftSight window. You can see the sheets came in fine from SketchUp. In the upper part of the graphics area I have an array of twelve title blocks with border. Starting with the one made in SketchUp I created a block and added text while deleting the outer border that was showing the edge of the paper. I made blocks of each of the floor plans and placed them on sheet A-2, Select > Copy > Edit > Paste as Block.

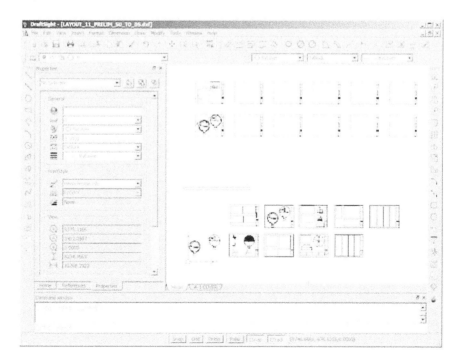

Configure DraftSight

To set the Units, Format > Unit system...

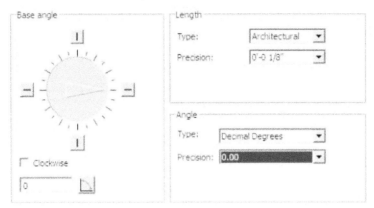

To set Dimensions, Format > Dimension Style > Dimension > Linear Dimension > Several settings:

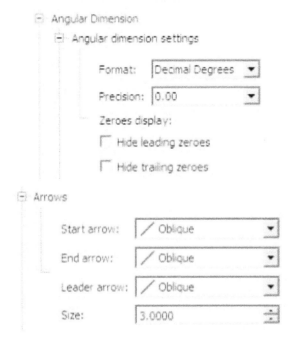

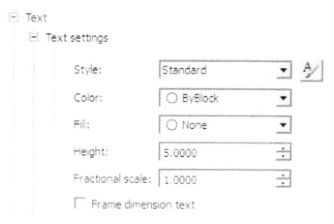

You may prefer other settings after trying these.

When you open the dxf from SketchUp, DraftSight will automatically place the sheets from SketchUp in the Model tab and insert a Sheet with a Viewport showing the entire layout. By resizing the Viewport you can zero in on the area you want on the first sheet, probably A-1. Zoom in so it fills the screen. Print from the Viewport, but do all the work in the Model tab.

A-1 COVER

Brought in as a referenced object was a Word document with a table for A-1, the cover sheet. It shows project parameters and team members with sheet index. It can be edited from within DraftSight by double clicking on it which opens Word in a new window. Please refer to the complete set of drawings at the end of the book.

AGENCIES	SITE PARAMETERS	BUILDING PARAMETERS	SHEET INDEX
BUILDING DEPARTMENT COCHISE COUNTY, AZ	SITE ADDRESS	PROJECT SUMMARY	A-1 COVER SHEET
		PRIVATE RESIDENCE MONOLITHIC DOME CONST THIN SHELLED, FERRO-CEMENT 5/8ths OBLATE SPHEROID, 38'D x 19'H	A-2 FLOOR PLANS, SITE PLAN
HEALTH DEPARTMENT	PROPERTY SETBACKS		A-3 ELEVATIONS
			A-4 FOUNDATION & FRAMING
WATER DEPARTMENT	ZONING	ONE BDRM, ONE FULL BATH MAIN FLOOR: 960 LOFT FLOOR: 412	A-5 ELECTRICAL
ARCHITECTURAL REVIEW		TOTAL: 1372 SQFT SURFACE AREA OF DOME: 2250 sf	A-6 PLUMBING
	ASSESSORS PARCEL NUMBER	VOLUME OF DOME: 12,764 cf LOT: 3.5 ACRES	A-7 ENERGY USAGE
ISLAND AUTHORITY	LEGAL DESCRIPTION	1 ACRE DEVELOPED	A-8 DOME & OPENINGS
			A-9 DOME NOTES
BUILDING CODE	AREA MAP	CONSULTANTS	A-10 CONSTRUCTION NOTES
ALL WORK SHALL COMPLY WITH THE 2007 INTERNATIONAL BUILDING CODE OR THE CODE WHICH HAS BEEN APPROVED AND ADOPTED BY THE CONTROLLING AUTHORITY	LOT AREA	STRUCTURAL ENGINEER	
		CIVIL ENGINEER	
		SOILS ENGINEER	
USE AND INTERPRETATION		ENERGY ANALYSIS	
THESE CONSTRUCTION DOCUMENTS SHALL BE USED AND INTERPRETED ACCORDING TO NOTES FOUND ON SHEET A-10		MECANICAL DESIGN	
			GENERAL CONTRACTOR
		LAND SURVEYOR	

Back in SketchUp in the Project Summary section you can find the floor areas by selecting the face of the circle used to Push/Pull the 3D outer dome shell. Look on the Entity Info palette in the Area box. Mine says about 962 sqft. which includes the 7" of dome all around. For the loft it says 412 sqft. which excludes the dome.

To get the approximate surface area and volume for this 5/8 oblate ellipsoid you can make use of the Advanced Dome Calculator found on Monolithic.com.

Oblate Ellipsoid

Major Radius:	18
Minor Radius:	15.5
Height:	15.5
Calculate...	
Diameter:	36
Ellipticity:	1.16
Circumference:	113.1
Floor Area:	1,017.88
Surface Area*:	1,850.1
Volume*:	10,518.02
Level:	5.4
Radius @ Level:	16.87
Area @ Level:	894.33
Stemwall:	3.5
Stemwall Surface Area:	395.84
Total Surface Area:	2,245.94

There is no stemwall and the calculator doesn't do 5/8 domes. From the equator down will be treated as a stemwall. To get the total area add the dome and stemwall surface areas getting 2250 sqft. Total volume is 12,764 cuft. The Calculator gives the floor area at the equator where our floor is 3.5' lower. To check accuracy I scaled the second floor deck to the sides and rear and trimmed with the outer shell. I found the area to be 444.34 x 2 = 888.68 sqft compared with 894.33 sqft with the Calculator. Pretty close. You can use the Sphere Calculator at calculatorfreeonline.com as another check.

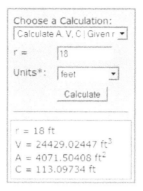

Our dome is not a perfect sphere and so will have less surface area and volume. The Dome Calculator gave an area above the equator of 1850 sqft and volume of 10,518 cuft. Close to the Sphere Calculator values divided by 2 at 2035 and 12,215. I'd say it checks. Fill in all the information you have on the Cover sheet.

3D view for the cover sheet. In SketchUp create a Scene called Exterior in which interior layers have been turned off. Click on Top view button. Use the Orbit tool to find a good angle adjusting the SketchUp window so only a small amount of space remains around the dome. Now, File > Export > 2D Graphic… save as a jpg after using the Option button to set the width to 800 pixels. In DraftSight position the image on your Cover sheet layout and scale to fit. Insert > Reference image… brings in the jpg of the 3D view.

A-2 FLOOR PLANS

Using DraftSight's drawing tools dimension and annotate both floor plans. With a more conventional house a corner might be chosen as the workpoint. For a dome it makes more sense to use the center as the workpoint. Whenever possible tie dimensions to the center point. The airform is unlikely to inflate perfectly. It will be lopsided, asymmetrical and can be off plus or minus a number of inches before you can send it back. Your dome constructor's first job after inflating the airform is to take enough measurements to determine how far from perfect it is. It is supposed to be 19' high. It could be 19'-3" or 18'-6". As the designer it is best to assume the shape will not be a perfect ellipsoid. Be careful not to over dimension. Do the minimum required to lock in your design.

A free program is certain to have a few bugs. DraftSight is no exception. After placing a dimension there is often a pause. The program locks up for up to thirty seconds. As a work-around till they fix it, try copying a dimension and adjust it to a new length instead of making a new dimension. This works very well with no lock up. Another problem is a polyline with arcs. The arcs may revert to straight lines on their own. Select > Double click a vertex and it will go back to arcs. Then Explode the polyline and it should stay put. Spline leaders may need the same treatment.

A-3 ELEVATIONS

Jpgs have been used for the four cardinal elevations. From SketchUp File > Export > 2D graphic. After scaling each one to approximately quarter inch scale, I used drafting tools to trace over the lines for the Right Elevation. Labels and text were also added.

A-4 RINGBEAM, FRAMING, DETAILS

The ringbeam and framing for the second floor can be combined in one drawing since neither is complicated. Three detail drawings have been place on this sheet. Notice at least one edge of each box has been lined up with another box edge. This insures a neat and tidy appearance. These details may later need to be updated to conform to the engineering sheets.

A-5 SITE PLAN, STAIR, ENTRY

The required Site Plan is found here along with several details. For each detail I returned to SketchUp and using Method 1 from Step 6 carefully sizing and positioning the grouped face to give me just the section needed.

A-6 ELECTRICAL

The Electrical sheet will require more time than the others. A lot of information is required. It takes a while to figure out the circuits and draw them, taking care that it all remains readable and accurate. How much can you put on one circuit? Do an online search for "Calculating Safe Circuit Loads". Here's what I found at about.com:

15-amp Circuit

Total Wattage Capacity: 15 amps x 120 volts = 1,800 watts

Safe Wattage Capacity: 1,800 watts x 80% = 1,440 watts

Safe Amperage Capacity: 15 amps x 80% = 12 amps

20-amp Circuit

Total Wattage Capacity: 20 amps x 120 volts = 2,400 watts

Safe Wattage Capacity: 2,400 watts x 80% = 1,920 watts

Safe Amperage Capacity: 20 amps x 80% = 16 amps

30-amp Circuit

Total Wattage Capacity: 30 amps x 120 volts = 3,600 watts

Safe Wattage Capacity: 3,600 watts x 80% = 2,880 watts

Safe Amperage Capacity: 30 amps x 80% = 24 amps

The bathroom fan, light, and heater should have a 20-amp circuit. Make all outlets in bathrooms GFCI's. Cover any lights with lenses or globes. Call for a moisture resistant fixture if in a shower or tub area. Provide plenty of light around the mirror, at the sides and/or along the top with the switch near the mirror. If the bathroom doesn't have an operable window, an exhaust fan must be provided. A nice feature is an electric heater with fan to take the chill off. An outlet is required within one foot of the sink with its own 20-amp circuit, but not over the sink. A quad outlet is not a bad idea.

In the kitchen provide a separate circuit for the microwave, refrigerator, garbage disposal, and dishwasher. A minimum of two receptacle circuits for the counter top area. An electric range, cook top, or oven must each have its own 240-volt circuit.

Place a wall switch beside the door of a bedroom, dining room or living room. That switch can either control a ceiling light, a wall light, or an outlet connected to a lamp. No pull chain allowed for ceiling lights. No more than 12' between receptacles to accommodate 6' cords. Dining rooms usually require a separate 20-amp circuit for one outlet used for a microwave, entertainment center, or window air conditioner.

Stairways require three-way switches at the top and bottom. Error on the side of safety to ensure all treads are well lighted.

Provide plenty of overhead lighting in any hallway. If ten feet or longer add a duplex outlet. A three way switch at both ends of the hallway is required, too. Consider four way switches if you have several bedroom doors that are separated.

A light is required in each closet, an overhead fixture with a globe for safety. An option is to place a single tube fluorescent over the door which tends to minimize shadows while providing good lighting.

The cloths washer and dryer will each have a dedicated circuit. An electric dryer requires a 240v circuit. In this design the washer and dryer are combined.

A garage should have at least one switch for the lighting, the door closer light doesn't count. Three way switches by the man door and the car door are a nice touch. One or more outlets are needed, make them GFCI for safety. Same for outdoor outlets, one by the front door and one by the side door of the weather proof type.

CIRCUITS FOR HOUSE, A Summary

BATHROOM - 20A DEDICATED FOR RECEPTICAL, GFI, NO LIGHTS

EXT. OUTLETS - 2 NEEDED, GFI

ONE CIRCUIT - TEN OUTLETS, MAX. IS SAFE

DINING ROOM - SEPARATE CIRCUIT

BEDROOM OUTLETS - AFCI, ARC FAULT CIRCUIT INTERRUPTOR

KITCHEN - 12" OR WIDER, COUNTER NEEDS AN OUTLET

KITCHEN - PENENSULA BAR 12" OR MORE, OUTLET NEEDED

KITCHEN - MIN. (2) 20A CIR. FOR OUTLETS, REFER OK

        NO GARBAGE DISP., HOOD, DW, TRASH COMP

        OR LIGHTING ON THESE TWO.

GFI REQUIRED - BATHROOM, OUTDOOR, GARAGE, KITCHEN COUNTER

        ANY AREA NEAR WATER, ~6'

AFCI REQ. - ALL ROOMS IN A HOUSE, EXCEPT

        BATHROOM, KITCHEN, LAUNDRY, GARAGE (GFI)

SEPERATE 20A - DISHWASHER, GARBAGE DISPOSAL, WASHING MACH.

SEPARATE CIR. - ALL 240V APPLIANCES

LIGHTING - 15A > 600 SQFT

LIGHTING - 20A > 800 SQFT

LIGHTING - MAX. OF TEN FIXTURES ON ONE CIRCUIT

        CEILING FAN W/LIGHT = ONE FIXTURE

MAX. LOAD FOR CIRCUIT - 80 % OR LESS THAN WATTAGE CAPACITY OF WIRE

        CAP.w = A x V = 15A X 120V = 1440W MAX.

        80% x 1440 = 1152W ALLOWED = 11 100W BULBS, E.G.

SMOKE DETECTORS - 120V WIRED W/ BATTERY BACKUP, AFCI

        ONE ON EVERY FLOOR

ONE OUTSIDE EVERY BEDROOM OR INSIDE, CHECK LOCAL REQUIREMENTS

STAIRWAYS, MAIN HALLWAYS, GARAGE, CHECK LOCAL REQUIREMENTS

FOR DOMES, ONE AT HIGH POINT.

GANG WIRED ALARMS, ONE GOES OFF THEY ALL GO

CARBON MONOXIDE (CO) DETECTOR - RECMMND: BEDROOM, MIN. IF USING ANY FUEL IN HOUSE Front Load Battery-Operated Carbon Monoxide Alarm with Digital Display

ELECTRIC HEATERS - 15A > 2880W, 20A > 3840W, 30A > 5760W

A-7 LOAD CALCULATIONS

If you have MS Excel a handy calculator spreadsheet can be found on Mike Holt's website: http://www.mikeholt.com/freestuff.php?id=freegeneral Scroll down to Residential Load Calculations. I printed the completed form as a pdf. Then, using a couple screen captures spliced together in the photo editing software, I converted it to jpg for import into the CAD program.

Another alternative is the online calculator called NEC Standard Method Single Family Residential - Electric Service Entrance Load Calculator. It can be found here: http://www.zenfixit.com/load_calculations.shtml. From that site an explanation of watts vs. volt-amps:

> **What's the Difference between Watts and Volt-Amps?** Volt-amps as the name implies = volts * amps, but watts also = volts * amps, so what is the difference? Volt-amp ratings represent a **maximum** value, whereas Watt ratings are more like an average value over time. For some appliances both ratings have the same value, and for others there is a large difference. Imagine an oven that draws lots of current while it is preheating, but then may use very little for several minutes at a time once it is heated up. When there is a difference then volt-amps will be the larger of the two, and the ratio of watts/volt-amps is called the **power factor,** and is represented as either a decimal (0.8) or a percentage (80%). Confused? Don't sweat it; just use which ever value is on the appliance name plate or the larger of the two in the rare case that both might be listed.

Also on this sheet is the Residential Lighting Worksheet required by the plan review agency. I have redrawing the table in the CAD program. The Service Entrance Diagram is another requirement.

A-8 PLUMBING & SECTIONS

Plumbing diagrams were done in Sketchup and brought into DraftSight as Blocks. Then the line type for hot water supply was changed to a dashed line.
The fixture units table was done in DraftSight. Fixture units are used to determine the pipe size for both supply and waste. Search for Table AP103.3(2) Load Values Assigned to Fixtures in the Building Code found at http://bulk.resource.org/codes.gov/bsc.ca.gov/gov.ca.bsc.2010.02.5.html .

Bathtub............1.4 Fixture Units

Clothes washer....1.4

Hose bib...........3.0

Lavatory...........0.7

Kitchen sink........1.4

Toilet...............2.2

Adding gives a total of 10.1 Fixture Units.

Once you have the total fixture units scroll down to Section AP201, Selection of Pipe Size... There you will find several charts which give the pipe size considering water pressure and length of pipe.

Now look for Drainage Fixture Unit Loads for Sanitary Piping to size the waste pipe. Label the diagrams showing pipe sizes.

HOT WATER HEATER NOTES:

QUICK DISCONNECT, CHECK LOCAL REQRMNTS

EARTHQUAKE STRAPPING, CHECK LOCAL REQRMNTS

PAN AND DRAIN TO APPROVED LOCATION, PROTECT HOUSE

PRESSURE/TEMPERATURE RELIEF LINE: AVOID BLOW UP

    TO APPROVED LOCATION, CHECK LOCAL REQRMNTS

EXPANSION TANK: MAY BE REQRD, CHECK

INSULATION: TANK R-24 MIN, JACKET OR BLANKET R-8, MIN.

INSULATION: HW PIPES, FOAM SLEEVES, ALL YOU CAN REACH

<u>GAS HEATER</u>: VENT SAFELY

STAND: MAY BE REQUIRED, CHECK

DRIP LEG: IN GAS LINE, MANU. MAY REQ.

BOLLARD OR BARRIER: PROTECT FROM CAR IN GARAGE.

<u>ELECTRIC HEATER</u>: IN UNHEATED SPACE

PLACE TANK ON INCOMPRESSABLE, INSULATED SURFACE

MIN. OF R-10, TO REDUCE HEAT LOSS.

The Sections are simply jpgs with annotations.

A-9 DOME OPENINGS

The dome constructor will want to know exactly where and what size the openings in the shell are and so will the engineer. Again, use the center workpoint. Show the degrees and distance for each opening. Include a note like this: All opening sizes are nominal. Confirm with owner the actual sizes prior to construction. Just in case we need to use a different window, for example. Monolithic also needs to know where the openings are to make the airlock in the best place and the inflation air tube.

This sheet also has the four elevations showing only the openings. The Dome Section was the first drawing we made in SketchUp. These key dimensions will be needed by the engineer, Monolithic and the dome constructor. The Side Entry Study was added here as well.

A-10 ENERGY USAGE

Will your building comply with energy code requirements? Find out with REScheck: http://www.energycodes.gov/rescheck/download.stm. To make these jpgs it was necessary to do two or more screen captures as large as possible and then assemble them in an image editing program. Since the sheet is nearly all jpgs this has resulted in the largest file for any of the sheets at 3 mb.

I've listed energy related features of the dome, plus site specific variables and dome parameters.

A-11 CONSTRUCTION NOTES

These are standard boiler plate specifications that could be used for any type of house construction. A larger project would have a separate set of

specifications in book form. On a smaller job like this one sheets A-11 and A-12 plus notes throughout the set are enough.

A-12 DOME NOTES

Dome notes are the specifications for Monolithic dome construction.

Step 9: Structural Engineering

A Set for the Engineer

When you are happy with the design and have decided to make no more changes you are ready to send a pdf set to the structural engineer. Publish a set in pdf and dwg. The dwg drawings can be used as a template by the engineer saving him time. His software may be able to open vector pdfs. Either way he will have the information he needs.

Can DraftSight export top quality pdfs? Yes, but with a problem. No matter what you use for the quality setting, DS always puts out a 15mb pdf for the cover sheet. The quality is very good, the file size is unacceptable. Sheet A-6 became an 8+ mb pdf. This is a known problem. Hopefully, by the time you read this it will have been fixed.

To deal with this it was necessary to employ a second free CAD program, DoubleCAD XT. The DraftSight dwg file open in DoubleCAD easily and look fine at first glance. The black background was changed to white. Then I began to notice some of the text was missing. Other text was shifted. After carefully examining each drawing and correcting all the errors I was ready to print to pdf from paper space. The twelve tabs came in from DraftSight with the Viewports ready to go. In Page Setup I selected 24x18" paper, ½" margins and 300 ppi for images. Then, the Viewport was scaled so that the margin line of the title block exactly matched the margin of the paper in the Viewport. The result was a very good set of vector pdfs! That 15 mb pdf became 185 kb! Much better. A-10, almost all images, was far larger that the others at 3 mb, not unexpected.

So, why not just use DoubleCAD instead of DraftSight? Because DoubleCAD is unable to save as a dwg or dxf at this writing. It saves fine in its native .2cd format. But the engineer won't be able to open it in AutoCAD. If he is happy with just the pdfs, then all is well. Nearly always CAD professionals provide either dwg or dxf. Check with your engineer. He may be able to convert a vector pdf to dwg with no problem. Or he may be going to redraw your floor plan and sections from scratch anyway and add his standard details.

A search for pdf to dxf converter shows that most are around two hundred dollars. The least expensive I found was Pdf 2 Dxf 2.0 at $49: http://www.cadkas.com/downengpdf11.php. I haven't tried it.

The free vector program called Inkscape opened the pdf for sheet A-4. Trying to save as a dxf did not work. After a few attempts it froze up. What did work was DrawPlus X4. It opened the sheet A-4, exported it as a dwg which then opened in

DraftSight with editable text and useable vector lines. DrawPlus is a good vector drawing program currently under $30 on buy.com.

The Engineering

The engineer will size all the structural parts of your design: The dome itself, the ringbeam, other footings, post, beams and joists. An attempt will be made to stick with the structure you have proposed and designed for, unless safety or efficiency mandates a deviation. He will send you a pdf set of his drawings. It is possible the Plan Review official will require a "wet stamped" set of structural sheets. That means a printed set the engineer has physically stamped and signed. Contractors and others will be happy with the sheets you have printed locally.

Study the engineering drawings carefully. Modify your drawings so they conform to the engineer's, if necessary. Having two different size ringbeams in the same set of drawings, for example, will be confusing and probably end up in extra charges.

Step 10: The Complete Set

Combining your corrected set with the engineering drawings makes the complete set. Now is the time to go back over the entire set to make sure everything is as complete and correct as you can make it. The best thing is to ask someone in the industry to review your plans and redline them. It's easy to work on drawings for weeks and months and overlook something that will be obvious to a fresh eye.

A way to get a fresh look is to print all the sheets. Many times things you missed will pop out on the printed page. You will be able to print the full 18x24" sheets on 8.5x11" paper using your home printer and still be able to read the text. If your printer can handle 11x17" paper, even better.

When all is in order publish a final version of your drawings in pdf. You can probably find a print shop like Kinko's within driving distance. Call to get their email address. Send everything in pdf format. Then call to confirm they have been received and order a test set. If all is well, have as many sets printed as you think you will need. Six sets might be enough for starters.

An alternative to the print shop is a store with a large format copier. Print out your sheets on your home printer. Explain that you want to print them as close to scale as you can. The percentage of enlargement can be adjusted until your quarter inch scale ruler says you are right on. Make a note of the percentage for future use.

When you hand out the sets of prints be sure to log the name and contact information of each plan holder. You will need this information for the next Step.

Step 11: Addendums

Addendums come in handy when you find out that your perfect set of drawings is actually not perfect. You might need to make an important change; the addendum is how you notify all plan holders. Send them out to everyone on your plan holders log., both email and hard copy Try to use just text, short and to the point. If needed for clarity, a drawing can be added. Follow up with a phone call to make sure it was received and understood.

Here's an example. Suppose you had a note on your drawings calling for egress windows in all bedrooms. But, you failed to notice that one window did not get updated and still shows a non-egress window. You get a call from the plan reviewer asking for clarification. Send out a hard copy of your addendum and ask everyone to staple it to the offending sheet and add a note about the Addendum on the sheet at each affected location.

ADDENDUM No. ONE (1)
to the
CONSTRUCTION DRAWINGS AND NOTES
fo construction of

THE _____ RESIDENTIAL PROJECT
for
THE CITY OF WILLCOX
COCHISE COUNTY, ARIZONA

February 11, 2011

Addendum No. One (1) covers the following changes to the contract documents and notes:

EGRESS WINDOWS

SHEET A-2 - FLOOR PLANS

Windows W02, W03 and W04, 3' by 3',
change to Andersen CXW14 400 Series Casement,
2'-11 15/16"w x 4'-0"h with clear width and height of 26.24" x 43.15"
and openable area of 7.86 sq. ft., or better.

Please mechanically affix this page to the appropriate sheet of the plans and
make a note on the sheet at each affected location that an Addendum has been issued.

Thank you.

_____
Robert Bissett, ISAP
Dome Design Specialist

Step 12: Shop Drawings

In several places on the working drawings shop drawings have been called for. This gives the dome constructor and contractor the opportunity to employ the newest and best materials and methods. Or at least those he is familiar with.

It is important to realize your areas of imperfect knowledge. You don't want to insist on a certain method or material that the contractor or dome constructor doesn't feel comfortable with. If you have committed to a general contractor rather than putting the project out for bid, you can ask how he would prefer to build a particular element. If a he has a way to flash and seal around the windows, for example, that he knows will work from experience, put that in your drawings to begin with.

If you will be going out to bid, add a note calling for a shop drawing that explains how each bidder proposes to flash and seal around the windows. You will probably get a different way from each one and learn a lot in the process. Either way you don't necessarily want to rule out alternate materials and methods.

It could be that the contractor submits a hand drawn sketch of his idea. To save time and money and to avoid any confusion you may want to draft up his drawing to scale yourself for his signature.

Below is a sample shop drawing from graitec.com. Graitec is a worldwide company supporting the construction industry. Actually this is just a part of the shop drawing for this set of stairs. There were other views and details. You can see that it is fully dimensioned and labeled. Their draftsmen would have used your working drawings of the stairs as a starting point. If this were a shop drawing for your project you would need to study it carefully before approving it. Once approved the drawing is sent to the shop to be manufactured.

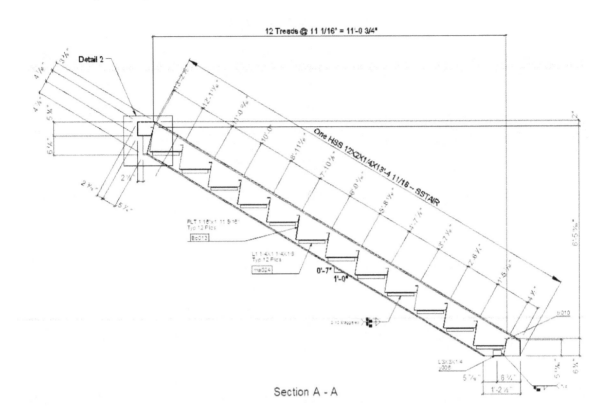

Section A - A

Working Drawings, A-1 to A-12

See links in Resources to download pdf and dwg files

DOME PROJECT

MODELED IN SKETCHUP, LAYOUT BY DRAFTSIGHT

COVER
PROJECT INFO
3D VIEW

A 001

SHEET INDEX

A-1   COVER, SITE PLAN
A-2   FLOOR PLANS
A-3   ELEVATIONS
A-4   RINGBEAM, FRAMING DETAILS
A-5   SITE PLAN, STAIR
A-6   ELECTRICAL
A-7   LOAD CALCULATIONS
A-8   PLUMBING & BLDG SECTIONS
A-9   ENERGY USAGE
A-10   DOME OPENINGS, DOME SECTION
A-11   CONSTRUCTION NOTES
A-12   DOME NOTES

GENERAL CONTRACTOR

BUILDING PARAMETERS

PROJECT SUMMARY

PRIVATE RESIDENCE
MONOLITHIC DOME CONST
THIN-SHELLED FERRO-CEMENT
5/8ths OBLATE SPHEROID 36'D x 19'H

ONE BDRM ONE FULL BATH
MAIN FLOOR 960
LOFT FLOOR 412
TOTAL 1372 SQFT
SURFACE AREA OF DOME 2250 sf
VOLUME OF DOME 12,764 cf
LOT 3.5 ACRES,
1 ACRE DEVELOPED

CONSULTANTS

STRUCTURAL ENGINEER

CIVIL ENGINEER

SOILS ENGINEER

ENERGY ANALYSIST

MECANICAL DESIGN

LAND SURVEYOR

SITE PARAMETERS

SITE ADDRESS

PROPERTY SETBACKS

ZONING

ASSESSORS PARCEL NUMBER

EASEMENTS

LOT INFO

LOT AREA

LEGAL DISCRIPTION

AGENCIES

BUILDING DEPARTMENT
COCHISE COUNTY, AZ

HEALTH DEPARTMENT

WATER DEPARTMENT

ARCHITECTURAL REVIEW

ISLAND AUTHORITY

BUILDING CODE

ALL WORK SHALL COMPLY WITH
THE 2007 INTERNATIONAL
BUILDING CODE OR THE CODE
WHICH HAS BEEN APPROVED AND
ADOPTED BY THE CONTROLLING
AUTHORITY

USE AND INTERPRETATION

THESE CONSTRUCTION DOCU-
MENTS SHALL BE USED AND
INTERPRETED ACCORDING TO
NOTES FOUND ON SHEET A-10

RENDERED OBJECT, WHEN ZOOL, DOUBLE CLICK TO EXIT

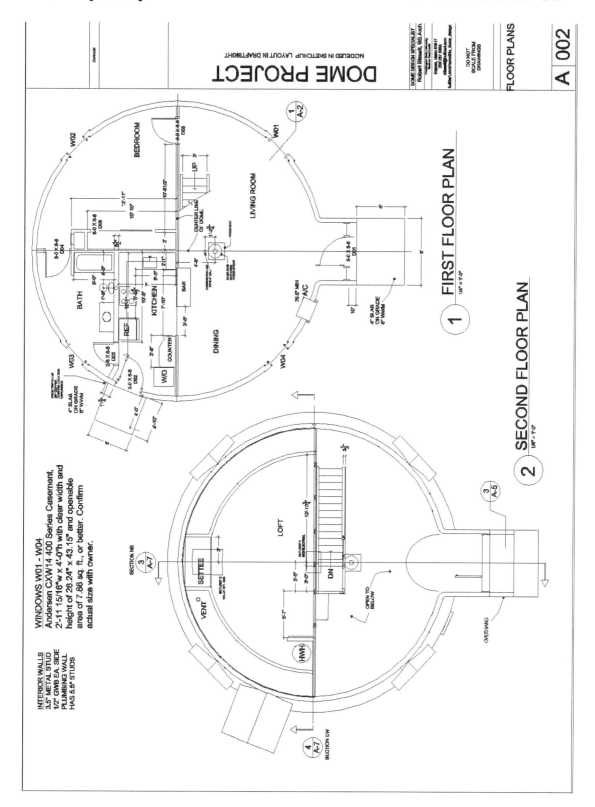

DOME PROJECT

MODELED IN SKETCHUP LAYOUT IN DRAFTSIGHT

DOME DESIGN SPECIALIST
Robert Bissett, BS Arch.

FLOOR PLANS

A 002

DO NOT
SCALE FROM
DRAWINGS

1 FIRST FLOOR PLAN
1/4" = 1'-0"

2 SECOND FLOOR PLAN
1/4" = 1'-0"

WINDOWS W01 - W04
Andersen CXW14 400 Series Casement,
2'-11 15/16"w x 4'-0"h with clear width and
height of 26.24" x 43.15" and openable
area of 7.86 sq. ft., or better. Confirm
actual size with owner.

INTERIOR WALLS
3.5" METAL STUD
1/2" GWB EA. SIDE
PLUMBING WALL
HAS 5.5" STUDS

BEDROOM

LIVING ROOM

DINING

KITCHEN

BATH

COUNTER

W/D

REF

BAR

LOFT

SETTEE

VENT

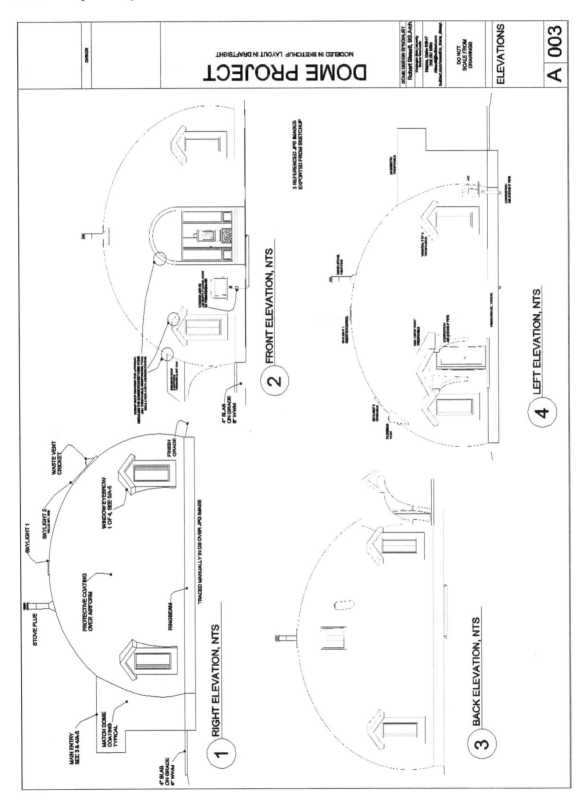

DOME PROJECT

MODELED IN SKETCHUP, LAYOUT IN DRAFTSIGHT

3 REFERENCED JPG IMAGES EXPORTED FROM SKETCHUP

DOME DESIGN SPECIALIST
Robert Bissett, BS Arch

ELEVATIONS

A 003

DO NOT SCALE FROM DRAWINGS

OWNER

1 RIGHT ELEVATION, NTS

2 FRONT ELEVATION, NTS

3 BACK ELEVATION, NTS

4 LEFT ELEVATION, NTS

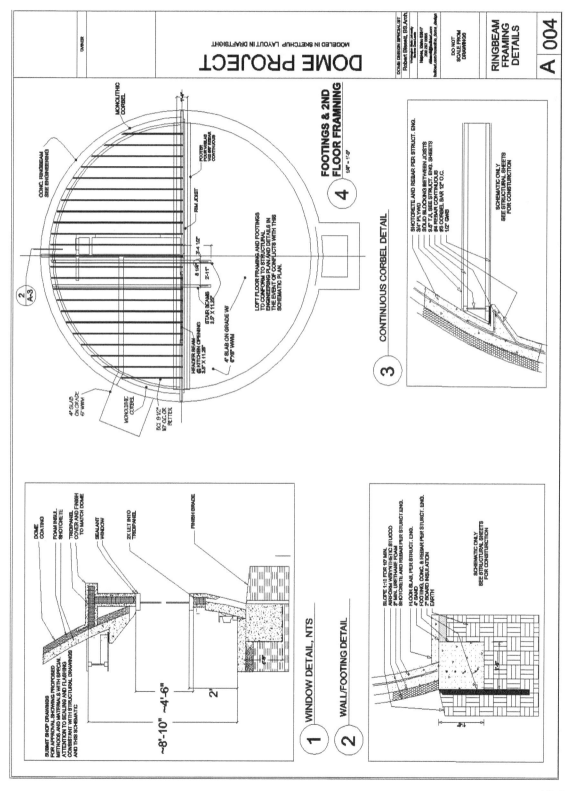

DOME PROJECT

MODELED IN SKETCHUP. LAYOUT IN DRAFTSIGHT.

OWNER

DOME DESIGN SPECIALIST
Robert Bissett, BS.Arch.

RINGBEAM FRAMING DETAILS

A 004

DO NOT SCALE FROM DRAWINGS

MONOLITHIC CORBEL

CONC. RINGBEAM SEE ENGINEERING

FOOTER FORM W/BAR V/B 6Φ REBAR CONTINUOUS

RIM JOIST

STAIR BEAMS 3.5" X 11.25"

HEADER BEAM @ KITCHEN OPENING 3.5" X 11.25"

4" SLAB ON GRADE W/ 6"X6" WWM

LOFT FLOOR FRAMING AND FOOTINGS TO CONFORM TO STRUCTURAL ENGINEERING PLAN AND DETAILS IN THE EVENT OF CONFLICTS WITH THIS SCHEMATIC PLAN.

4" SLAB ON GRADE 6" WWM

MONOLITHIC CORBEL

5CI 9 1/2" 12" O.C. OR BETTER

(4) FOOTINGS & 2ND FLOOR FRAMING 1/4" = 1'-0"

(3) CONTINUOUS CORBEL DETAIL

SHOTCRETE AND REBAR PER STRUCT. ENG.
3/4" PLYWD
SOLID BLOCKING BETWEEN JOISTS
9.5" T.J.I, SEE STRUCT. ENG. SHEETS
#4 REBAR CONTINUOUS
#5 CORBEL BAR 12" O.C.
1/2" GWB

SCHEMATIC ONLY SEE STRUCTURAL SHEETS FOR CONSTRUCTION

(1) WINDOW DETAIL, NTS

DOME COATING
FOAM INSUL SHOTCRETE
TRIDIPANEL COVER AND FINISH TO MATCH DOME
SEALANT
WINDOW
2X LET INTO TRIDIPANEL
FINISH GRADE

~8'-10" ~4'-6"
2'

SUBMIT SHOP DRAWINGS FOR APPROVAL SHOWING PROPOSED METHODS AND MATERIALS WITH SPECIAL ATTENTION TO SEALING AND FLASHING CONSISTENT WITH STRUCTURAL DRAWINGS AND THIS SCHEMATIC

(2) WALL/FOOTING DETAIL

SLOPE 1:10 FOR 10" MIN.
AIRFORM W/SYNTHETIC STUCCO
2" MIN. URETHANE FOAM
SHOTCRETE AND REBAR PER STRUCT. ENG.
FLOOR SLAB, CONC. & REBAR PER STURCT. ENG.
4" SAND
FOOTING, CONC. & REBAR PER STRUCT. ENG.
2" BOARD INSULATION
EARTH

SCHEMATIC ONLY SEE STRUCTURAL SHEETS FOR CONSTRUCTION

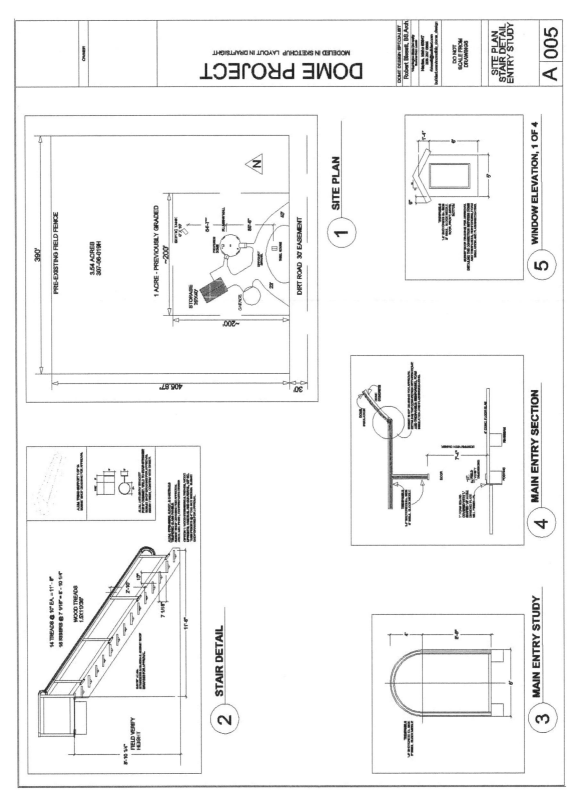

DOME PROJECT

MODELED IN SKETCHUP. LAYOUT IN DRAFTSIGHT

SITE PLAN
STAIR DETAIL
ENTRY STUDY

A 005

1 — SITE PLAN

5 — WINDOW ELEVATION, 1 OF 4

4 — MAIN ENTRY SECTION

3 — MAIN ENTRY STUDY

2 — STAIR DETAIL

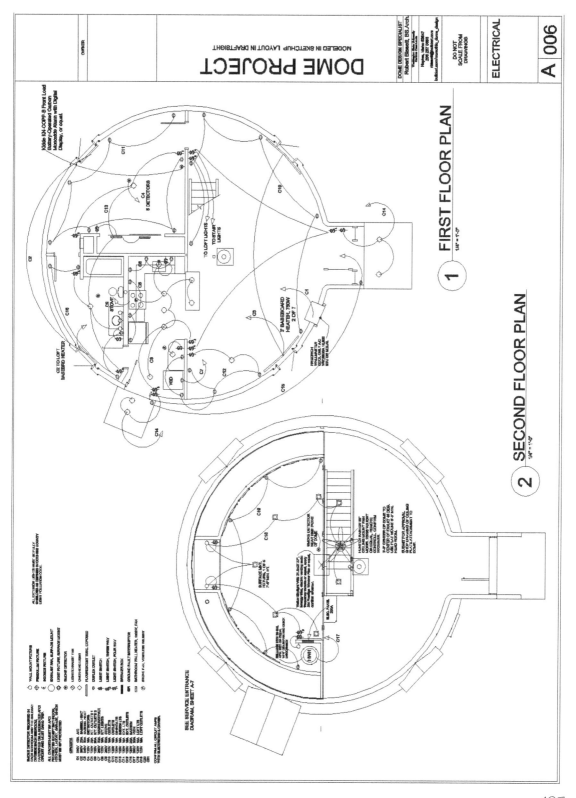

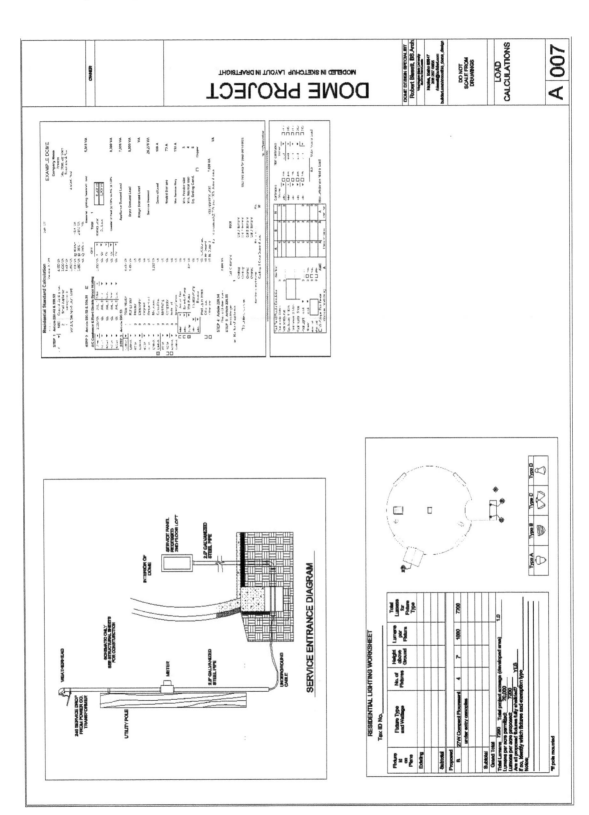

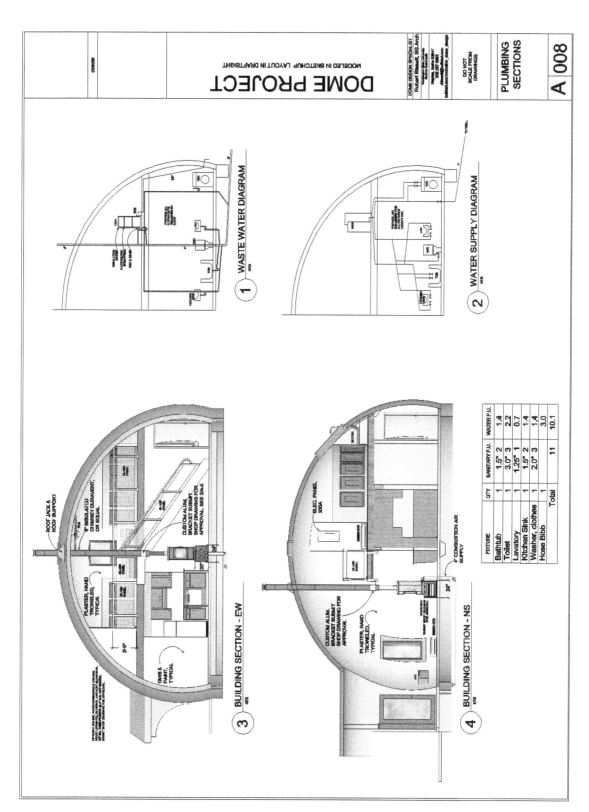

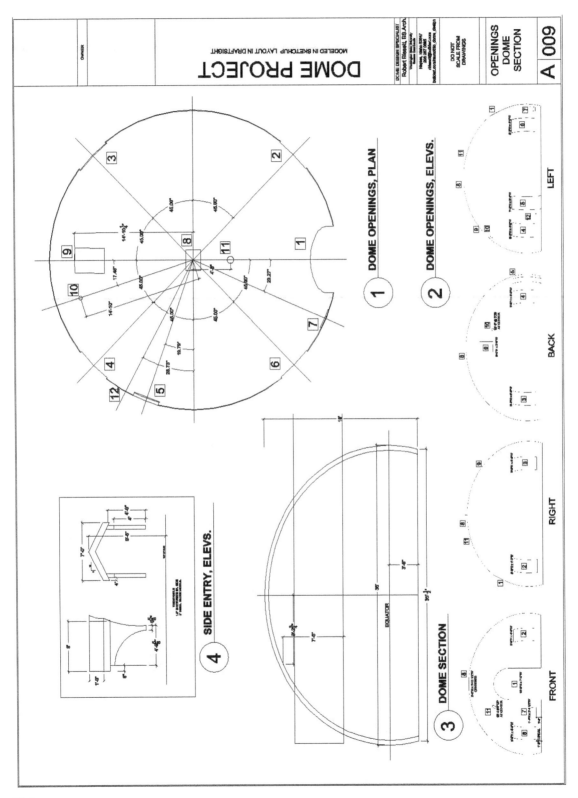

DOME PROJECT

MODELED IN SKETCHUP LAYOUT IN DRAFTSIGHT

DOME OPENINGS, PLAN

DOME OPENINGS, ELEVS.

DOME SECTION

SIDE ENTRY, ELEVS.

LEFT

BACK

RIGHT

FRONT

DOME DESIGN SPECIALIST
Robert Bissell, BS Arch.

DO NOT
SCALE FROM
DRAWINGS

OPENINGS
DOME
SECTION

A 009

DOME PROJECT

MODELED IN SKETCHUP LAYOUT IN DRAFTSIGHT

OWNER

DOME DESIGN SPECIALIST
Robert Bissett, BS Arch

DO NOT
SCALE FROM
DRAWINGS

ENERGY
USAGE

A 010

REScheck Software Version 4.4.1

Compliance Certificate

Project Title: Dome Project

2009 IECC
Willcox, Arizona
Single Family

2009 IECC Energy Efficiency Certificate

Insulation Rating	R-Value
Ceiling / Roof	0.00
Wall	60.00
Floor / Foundation	4.00
Ductwork (unconditioned spaces):

Glass & Door Rating	U-Factor	SHGC
Window	1.80	0.30
Skylight	0.55	0.30
Door	0.27	NA

Heating & Cooling Equipment	Efficiency
Heating System:
Cooling System:
Water Heater:

Name: _____ Date: _____
Comments:

ENERGY USAGE

NORMAL MAX TEMPERATURE: 96 DEGREES
NORMAL MIN TEMPERATURE: 27 DEGREES
HEATING DEGREE DAYS: 1424
COOLING DEGREE DAYS: 3266

DOME SHELL EFFECTIVE R VALUE: R60
DOCUMENTATION AVAILABLE

DOME SURFACE AREA: 2244 SQ. FT.
AVERAGE SHELL THICKNESS: 4.5"
YARDS OF CONCRETE IN SHELL: 30
THERMAL MASS OF SHELL: 60 TONS
SHELL INSULATION 3" URATHANE = R21
WINDOWS + SKYLIGHT = ~100 SQ. FT.

DESIGN LOSS = ~10,000 BTU/HR
BASEBOARD HEATERS:
(12) 36" HEATERS @ 1921 BTU/563 W
= 23,000 BTU/6560 W
AIRCONDITIONER = 15,800 BTU A-9

ANDERSEN ECOEXCEL 400 SERIES WINDOWS (0.3 SHGC OR EQUAL

AND THURMATRU FIBERGLASS INSULATED EXTERIOR DOORS (0.27 U FACTOR) OR EQUAL

AND VELLUX SKYLIGHT VSE 21.5X27.37", ENERGY STAR, ELECTRIC VENTING RADIO FREQ. REMOTE OR EQUAL.

3M PRESTIGE WINDOW FILM ON INTERIOR OF ALL GLASS SURFACES, WINDOWS AND SKYLIGHT.

ENERGY STAR APPLIANCES: REFRIGERATOR, STOVE, HOT WATER HEATER.

CEILING FAN TO AVOID STRATIFICATION OF AIR. OPERABLE SKYLIGHT AND WINDOWS COOL DOME AT NIGHT BY GRAVITY FLOW, THE "CHIMNEY EFFECT."

DOME PROJECT

MODELED IN SKETCHUP LAYOUT IN DRAFTSIGHT

OWNER

DOME DESIGN SPECIALIST
Robert Bissett, BS Arch

DO NOT SCALE FROM DRAWINGS

CONSTRUCTION NOTES

A 011

IN THE EVENT FURTHER
CLARIFICATION, EXPLANATION, DETAILS,
DIMENSIONS, ETC. SHOULD PROVE
NECESSARY DO NOT HESITATE TO
CONTACT THE DESIGN PROFESSIONAL. A
PHONE CALL IS OFTEN ENOUGH OR A
NEW DRAWING IN PDF OR JPG FORMAT
SENT BY EMAIL VIEWABLE IN THE FIELD.

ROBERT BISSETT
208 287 0685 OFFICE
208 597 1404 CELL
rbissett@builddirt.com

DOME PROJECT

MODELED IN SKETCHUP LAYOUT IN DRAFTSIGHT

OWNER

DOME DESIGN SPECIALIST
Robert Blissett, BS Arch.

DO NOT SCALE FROM DRAWINGS

DOME NOTES

A 012

SPECIAL CONSTRUCTION NOTES

PERFORMANCE SPECIFICATION FOR THIN-WALLED, FERRO-CONCRETE DOME STRUCTURE.

PART 1 – GENERAL

RELATED DOCUMENTS:
DRAWINGS AND GENERAL PROVISIONS OF THE CONTRACT, INCLUDING GENERAL CONDITIONS AND DIVISION 1 SPECIFICATION SECTIONS APPLY TO WORK SPECIFIED IN THIS SECTION.

DESCRIPTION OF WORK:
EXTENT OF CAST-IN-PLACE CONCRETE DOME IS SHOWN ON THE DRAWINGS. ALL DOMES SHALL BE CONSTRUCTED AND DESIGNED TO MEET THE REQUIREMENTS OF CONSTRUCTION AS DESCRIBED IN THE LATEST EDITION OF THE UNIFORM BUILDING CODE.

TYPE: A FREE-SPAN REINFORCED CONCRETE DOME INCLUDING RING BEAM FOUNDATION. DESIGN THE CONCRETE DOME SHALL BE DESIGNED IN ACCORDANCE WITH THE LATEST EDITION OF THE UNIFORM BUILDING CODE...

QUALITY ASSURANCE...

WARRANTY...

PART 2 – MATERIALS AND METHODS:

RING BEAM FOUNDATION...

SHOTCRETE...

Conclusion

That's the entire process with each step explained. With a little extra effort and a work around or two, it is possible to produce a professional set of working drawings entirely with free programs, saving thousands of dollars in software alone.

As you can see it's not really over when you print the final set. The drawings will likely change and expand until the project is completed. You're not done with them even then. A set should stay with the house in case questions arise in the future about how something was built. As the creator of your set of working drawings you own the copyright and could sell a set to someone to build another dome just like it. The engineer owns the copyright for the structural sheets. I wouldn't advise selling those. The engineering would probably need to be reviewed and reissued for any new building site.

The method described will work just as well for other types of construction, not just Monolithic domes.

I wish you the best on your project. Yes, it's a lot of work. With determination and diligence you can produce a great set of working drawings.

Robert Bissett
rbissett@buildart.com

Resources

Check my website for the links listed below: buildart.com/dome_diy.

Files

SketchUp file at 3dwarehouse.com. Search for Dome DIY.

DraftSight file: buildart.com/dome_diy

DoubleCAD XT file: buildart.com/dome_diy

Pdf version here: buildart.com/dome_diy

Software

Google SketchUp, 3D modeling, cost: free.

http://sketchup.google.com/intl/en/index.html

Google SketchUp Pro 30 day trial, cost: free.

http://sketchup.google.com/product/gsup.html

SU Plugin: Export Dxf, cost: free/donation

http://rhin.crai.archi.fr/rld/plugin_details.php?id=774

SU Plugin: Dxf In, cost: free/donation

http://forums.sketchucation.com/viewtopic.php?t=31186

SU Plugin: Flaten to Plane, cost: free/donation

http://modelisation.nancy.archi.fr/rld/plugin_details.php?id=753

SU Plugin: Unfold Tool, cost: free/donation

http://sketchuptips.blogspot.com/2007/08/plugin-unfoldrb.html

Dassaults Systemes DraftSight, 2D drafting, cost: free.

http://www.3ds.com/products/draftsight/free-cad-software/

DoubleCAD XT, 2D CAD, print pdf, cost: free

http://www.doublecad.com/Products/DoubleCADXTv3/tabid/1100/Default.aspx

WinTopo, convert .jpg to vector drawing, cost: free.

http://wintopo.com/

Gimp, Image manipulation, cost: free.

http://www.gimp.org/downloads/

AbiWord, word processing, cost: free.

http://www.abisource.com/

Using the above free software you will save many thousands of dollars. Here's some other software that may be of interest, some free, some inexpensive.

A9CAD, 2D CAD, cost: free

http://www.a9tech.com/a9cad

Kerkythea Renderer & SketchUp plugin, cost: free

http://www.sketchupartists.org/tutorials/sketchup-and-kerkythea/architectural-rendering-with-sketchup-and-kerkythea/

SketchUp Styles 2011, cost: free

http://www.sketchupartists.org/2011/02/styles-2011/

Blender, 3D modeling, cost: free.

http://www.blender.org/

Bryce 7, 3D visualization, landscape, rendering, cost: $29.95

http://www.daz3d.com/i/shop/itemdetails/?item=11035&trid=201415921

DrawPlus X4, vector drawing, open pdf, cost $30: search for best price

http://www.serif.com/drawplus/

Qcad, 2D CAD, cost: $34.02

http://www.qcad.org/qcad.html

TurboCAD Designer 18, 2D CAD, cost: $39.99

http://www.turbocad.com/TurboCAD/TurboCADWindows/TurboCADDesigner18/tabid/1626/Default.aspx?gclid=COfwpYTQsagCFQ12gwodROM3DQ

TurboCAD Deluxe 18, 2D/3D CAD, cost: $129.99

http://www.turbocad.com/TurboCAD/TurboCADWindows/TurboCADDeluxe18/tabid/1869/Default.aspx

Useful Sites

Google SketchUp Community, cost: free

http://sketchup.google.com/intl/en/community/

3D Warehouse, models, cost: free

http://sketchup.google.com/3dwarehouse/details?mid=cef32ff5bc8ca875744c98eb42eda842&ct=mdsa

Sketchucation, forums, plugins, news, etc., cost: free

http://forums.sketchucation.com/

Ruby Library Depot, plugins, cost: free/donation

http://modelisation.nancy.archi.fr/rld/index.php

Monolithic Dome, ideas, info, forum, airform

http://www.monolithic.com/

Building Code Online, cost: free

http://bulk.resource.org/codes.gov/bsc.ca.gov/gov.ca.bsc.2010.02.5.html

Useful Info

SketchUp Video Tutorials, cost: free

http://sketchup.google.com/training/videos.html

BUILDING STAIRS IN SKETCHUP

http://www.finehomebuilding.com/item/15911/stairmathter-use-sketchup-to-master-the-math-for-stairbuilding

DIGITAL JOB SITE

http://www.finehomebuilding.com/blog/digital-job-site

HASE-BARI WOOD STOVE

http://www.hearthstonestoves.com/wood-stoves/stove-details?product_id=27

CONDAR ASV-90 AIR SUPPLY VENTILATOR 4" PIPE DOWN LOW

http://www.condar.com/asv.html

VELUX_GPL_M08 30 5/8" X 55"; RO 31 ¼" X 55 ½"

http://www.theskylightstore.com/GetPricing.aspx?ProductCategory=Roof_Windows&ProductType=Top_Hinged

GOOD INFO FROM A HOME INSPECTOR

http://www.bradyinspects.com/home-info.html

PLUMBING 10 COMMON MISTAKES.

http://www.finehomebuilding.com/PDF/Free/021126070.pdf

Books

A Manual of Construction Documentation, Glen Wiggins, Whitney Library of Design, Watson-Guptill.

Architictural Working Drawings, Residential & Commercial, W. Spence, Wiley & Sons.

Monolithic's Book Resources

http://www.monolithic.com/topics/book

Google SketchUp for Dummies, Chopra
Amazon.com

Appendix

The typical set of working drawings includes:

Site Plans

Floor Plans

Roof Plans

Reflected Ceiling Plans

Exterior Elevations

Building Sections

Wall Sections

Vertical Transportation

Enlarged Plans and Interior Elevations

Schedules

Details

In a smaller building like this dome it is possible to include all important information by combining drawings. For example, Reflected Ceiling Plan information can be found on the various floor plans. Enlarged Plans were not needed, nor were separate Interior Elevations, though the building sections include some interior elevations. If your plan includes a custom feature, say a built in bookcase, then be sure to add an elevation and enlarged plan describing exactly what you have in mind. Often the cabinet supplier will design the kitchen for you.

In this dome we have only four windows and two skylights. I have noted on the plans what those are to be. In a larger building you would add a Schedule sheet showing each window frame type. Similarly, a door schedule may have a line for each door giving it's number, type, material, width, height, thickness, frame type, frame material, detail references for the strike, hinge, head and sill, hardware group number and remarks.

Finish schedules have a line for each room showing room number, room name, material and finish of the floor, the base, each wall, ceiling and remarks. Also a reference section is added with abbreviations for the schedule entries. Below are some examples from a recent dome project.

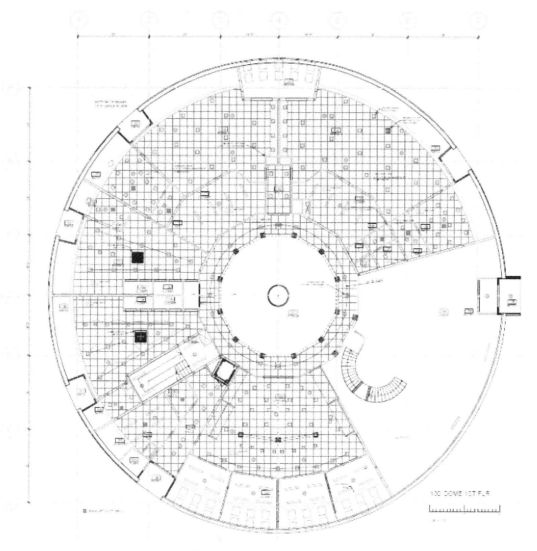

Reflected Ceiling Plan, example.

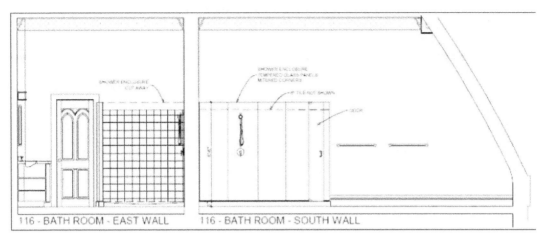

116 - BATH ROOM - EAST WALL   116 - BATH ROOM - SOUTH WALL

Interior Elevations, example.

| ANDERSEN DOOR & WINDOW SCHEDULE |||||||
MAY 12, '04						
RM	DR	CLAD?	QNTY	TYPE		R.O.
					DOORS	
109	EX01	ALUM	1	G	Patio, 400 Series – In swing	6'-0" x 6'-11" R.O.
110	EX02	"	1	G	Typical all Alum clad	6'-0" x 6'-11" R.O.
118	EX03	"	1	G		6'-0" x 6'-11" R.O.
118	GH04	WOOD	1	G	Similar to FWH60611PALR	6'-0" x 6'-11" R.O.
119	GH05	"	1	G	400 Series, Frenchwood Hinged Patio Door, in swing, no cladding	6'-0" x 6'-11" R.O.
119	EX06	ALUM	1	G		6'-0" x 6'-11" R.O.
213	EX07	WOOD	1	G		6'-0" x 6'-11" R.O.

Door Schedule, example.

					WINDOWS	
118	W01	WOOD	1	T	CXW16 - Fixed	3'-0 1/2" x 6'-0 3/8" R.O.
119	W02	"	1	T	"	"
213	W03	"	2	T	"	"
213	W04	"	2	T	"	"
301	W05	ALUM	1	S	Similar to CW24 – Operable	4'-9" x 4'-0 1/2" R.O.
301	W06	"	1	S	Or bigger, Arch. Series.	
301	W07	"	1	W	CIR20? CONFIRM	2'-0 5/8" R.O.
301	W08	"	1	W		
301	W09	"	1	W	"	"
301	W10	"	1	W		"

Window Schedule, example.

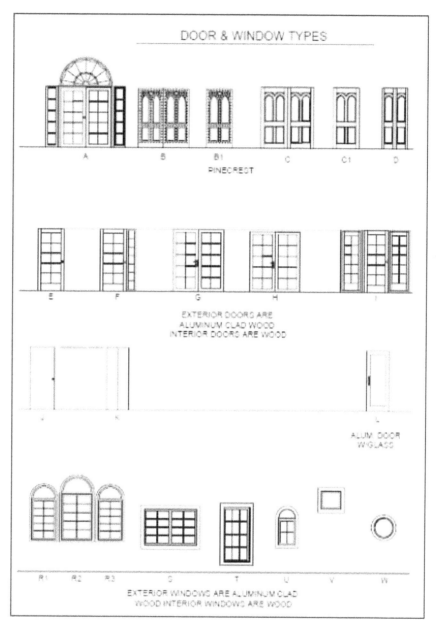

Door and window types, example.

AFTERWORD

Monolithic Domes are still a secret for the most part in today's world, but they date back centuries with the Pantheon in Rome being the oldest Dome built in 126 AD. Actually, there are some rock domes built in 5000 BC that are in Ireland but not using cement.

Light-frame construction, wide spread today, is a relatively recent innovation dating back to the early 19th century. Made possible with the advent of inexpensive machine-made nails and water powered sawmills; it was a cheaper and faster alternative to post and beam construction. While adequate for benign conditions, frame buildings are not able to withstand the extremes of nature. Who has not seen video of entire neighborhoods reduced to piles of jackstraw lumber and garbage? Painful to watch, imagine what it must be like to experience. The loss of property is regrettable; the loss of a loved one is devastating. All the more tragic because it does not need to happen.

Monolithic Dome houses have survived hurricane force winds, storm surges, earthquakes, forest fires and tornadoes and protected those inside. Imagine two families on adjacent lots. One lives in a standard wood frame house built to code and the other lives in a Monolithic Dome. They both notice a tornado headed in their direction. Who will seek shelter in the other's house? Who suddenly feels exposed and vulnerable? Two hundred mile per hour plus winds have a way of focusing the mind. Frame construction is a gamble and your odds are pretty good that you will not be the big loser. But, it's a risk you need not take. The square foot cost for a dome is comparable to a frame built custom home.

Here is a story that illustrates the incredible strength of a dome shell. Some years ago, a group in Colorado built a small dome about 60' in diameter, 30' high and 2" thick. It had windows, a door and a large opening, about 40' wide, on one side. After several years of use, the owners decided to sell the property. But the new owner wasn't interested in keeping the Dome, so he hired a local contractor to remove it. After inspecting the Dome, the contractor said that he could remove it in less than a day. His plan was to use a large front-end loader to lift the dome on the side opposite its wide entrance causing the dome to collapse. The concrete could than be broken up and hauled away. When he actually tried, it didn't work. His heavy equipment could not lift the side of the Dome. The contractor then brought up his crane with a large steel wrecking ball meaning to knock down the Dome in short order. After hours of pounding, the Dome, looking like a giant piece of Swiss cheese, was still standing. In the end it took more than a week to remove the Dome.

People living in a Monolithic Dome find that it is infinitely quieter than any other house; you just don't get the sound from outside. There are no drafts, the building itself is absolutely air tight, only the doors and windows will let in air. There is no such thing as enough snow to cause the Monolithic Dome any trouble. In fact, many Monolithic Domes have been buried in the ground up to thirty feet.

Located in Italy, Texas, Monolithic has been making Airforms and constructing these amazing buildings for more than thirty years. We are devoted to broadening the awareness and understanding of this technologically superior construction process through education. That is why we are excited to see that Real Working Drawings, Monolithic Dome Edition, is now available to the public. By guiding the reader through the building of a Dome in 3D on the computer the innovative becomes familiar. The home owner will know how one is put together. Producing one's own working drawings will not only save money, but increase knowledge of the entire construction process, a good thing when dealing with plan reviewers and contractors. Robert's logical, step by step approach and clear writing style puts the architects' craft within reach of the average person. We hope that many will come to hear of Domes as a result of this book and that many will realize the dream of Dome living. We invite you to stop by our extensive website www.monolithic.com.

David B. South,
President, Monolithic Dome Institute

Index

About the Author

Robert Bissett has been specializing in Monolithic dome design for over ten years. He has a degree in architecture from Washington State University, Summa Cum Laude, 1975. He has a degree in science from the United States Air Force Academy, 1967. In 1972, after five years as a pilot, two in Viet Nam flying helicopters and Caribous, he earned his FAA Airline Transport Rating. When not designing domes, Bob is an artist, author, blogger and teacher.

The photo above shows Dome of a Home in Pensacola Beach, Florida about two months after it survived hurricane Ivan in 2004. It was designed to withstand a sixteen foot storm surge. The stairs were torn away as expected and the five foot squares making up the garage floor were washed away. The dome was intact and functional when many stick frame houses were destroyed or badly damaged. Bob's life partner Loi Eberle is on the left. Mark Sigler, owner and visionary behind this design, is on the right.

Bob's dome brochure online is found here: http://www.buildart.com/monolithic_dome_design.htm. For more rectangular designs see http://www.buildart.com/architectural_design.htm. See original art on his website: buildart.com. For high quality fine art prints on paper and canvas see his galleries: http://robert-bissett.artistwebsites .com/?tab=artworkgalleries. For his five star art instructional book called Real Art Real Easy go to amazon: http://www.amazon .com/Real-Art-Easy-Yourself-Better/ dp/144 9900054.